PENNSYLVANIA FIRESIDE TALES

VOLUME 8

JEFFREY R. FRAZIER

CATAMOUNT
PRESS

an imprint of Sunbury Press, Inc.
Mechanicsburg, PA USA

CATAMOUNT
PRESS

an imprint of Sunbury Press, Inc.
Mechanicsburg, PA USA

For information about special discounts for bulk purchases, please contact Sunbury Press Orders Dept. at (855) 338-8359 or orders@sunburypress.com.

To request one of our authors for speaking engagements or book signings, please contact Sunbury Press Publicity Dept. at publicity@sunburypress.com.

FIRST CATAMOUNT PRESS EDITION: May 2025

Set in Adobe Garamond | Interior design by Crystal Devine | Cover by Lawrence Knorr | Edited by Debra Reynolds.

Publisher's Cataloging-in-Publication Data
Names: Frazier, Jeffrey R., author.
Title: Pennsylvania fireside tales volume 8 / Jeffrey R. Frazier.
Description: First trade paperback edition. | Mechanicsburg, PA : Catamount Press, 2025.
Summary: Volume 8 in the Pennsylvania Fireside Tales series exploring the origins and foundations of old-time Pennsylvania mountain folktales, legends, and folklore.
Identifiers: ISBN : 979-8-88819-305-1 (paperback).
Subjects: NATURE / Ecosystems & Habitats / Mountains | HISTORY / United States / State & Local / Middle Atlantic (DC, DE, MD, NJ, NY, PA) | FICTION / Fairy Tales, Folk Tales & Mythology.

Designed in the USA
0 1 1 2 3 5 8 13 21 34 55

For the Love of Books!

Cover: An interpretation of *Home, Sweet Home*, by Winslow Homer, circa 1863.

To my wife Helen, who passed in January 2018. May you find as much peace, beauty, and pleasure in Heaven as you did when you were my ever-present traveling companion during our explorations of Pennsylvania's little-traveled byways and locales where I found my legends. The mountains and I will always love you, fondly remember our many trips together, and never forget your smiling face and your enthusiastic love of the backwoods that matched my own in so many ways.

— ALSO BY —
JEFFREY R. FRAZIER

Pennsylvania Fireside Tales Volume I

Pennsylvania Fireside Tales Volume II:
The Black Ghost of Scotia & More Pennsylvania Fireside Tales

Pennsylvania Fireside Tales Volumes III, IV, V, VI, and VII

Ghosts of Penn's Woods

Pennsylvania Fireside Ghost Tales
(ghost tales from in and around Pennsylvania's state parks and historic sites)

Pennsylvania Mountain Landmark Volumes I–III

Madonna of the Trail. Located on U.S. Route 40 across from the Nemacolin Country Club near Beallsville, Washington County, this monument is one of a series of 12 commissioned by the National Society of Daughters of the American Revolution. They were placed along the old National Highway and extended from Bethesda, Maryland, to Upland, California. A fitting memorial to pioneer mothers of covered wagon days, but also a reminder of Pennsylvania's pioneer mothers of an even earlier time.

CONTENTS

Oral traditions may well exasperate the historian of a literate, or at least print-glutted society, with their quick-silver quality and chronological slipperiness. But they can be trapped, and they offer the chief available records for the beliefs and concerns and memories of large groups of obscured Americans. The historian can find history alive in the field as well as entombed in the library.

—Richard Dorson

Remember the days of old,
think of the generations long ago;
ask your father to recount it and your elders to tell you
the tale.

—Deuteronomy 32:7

INTRODUCTION

Once again, I seem to be making a liar of myself. I mentioned in all honesty in my *Pennsylvania Fireside Tales Volume VII* that I felt that it was definitely the last one in the seven-volume series, thinking that I had run out of tales I wanted to share with my readers. However, the types of stories that so fascinated me in the past seemed to keep seeking me out and to be crying out for an appearance on the printed page.

This in turn caused the compulsion I had always had to share them with my readers, to flare up and inspire me. Consequently, I published revised and expanded editions of my *Volumes I, II, III, V, VI and VII* which contained those new tales that trickled in to me since those editions first appeared.

In those revised editions I kept the volume numbers the same, even though I had added appreciable new details to many of the original tales that were in the first editions and also had added new chapters that were not in the first editions. I was proceeding along that same path with my *Volume IV*, it being the last volume for which I had not yet published a revised/expanded edition, but I was not enthused about the project.

Even though I had collected some additional material for some of *Volume IV*'s chapters and was moving toward a second edition, I had noticed that people seemed not inclined to buy my second editions if they already had the first editions, apparently thinking they already had that volume number in their collections.

Then, in the last year, I started to find many more new legendary tales and fascinating details that, coupled with the revised/expanded chapters from *Volume IV* that I already had in place for a revised/expanded *Volume IV* edition, would warrant the publication of an eighth volume.

The additions to the four *Volume IV* tales found herein include interesting details that were not discovered until after the earlier edition was published and which I felt needed to be added to the chapters in order to enhance their quality. In addition, this new *Volume VIII* has many new photos not included in any of my previous volumes.

I also have to say that after all these years (over 50 now) of collecting and writing Pennsylvania's old-time mountain folktales and legends, my related pleasurable experiences continue to grow. I can now, for instance, enthusiastically claim that in my many excursions throughout the state (which are still ongoing even as I approach 80) I have walked on the same soil, and perhaps in the very footsteps, of those who figured prominently in the state's history: people like captive Mary Jemison; Confederate General Robert E. Lee; Father of Pennsylvania Forestry Joseph Trimble Rothrock; highwayman Davy Lewis; Pennsylvania old-time great hunters of the wolf and mountain lion like Sam Askey, Laroy Lyman and Aaron Hall; and defenders of Pennsylvania's Colonial frontier like Colonel John Kelly, Samuel Brady, and Peter Pence.

Likewise, I can also claim that over this same half century of collecting tales here in Pennsylvania I've heard some almost-forgotten calls of the wild. Not too far from my parents' country homestead, in Potter Township of Centre County, there was for a time an elk farm where the owner raised some magnificent specimens of that big game animal.

It was always a treat to visit there in the springtime when it was not unusual to hear the bulls bugling during mating season. The shrill calls always served as thrilling reminders that Pennsylvania was once home to many big-game animals like this in the days before the lumber kings destroyed their habitat.

That same thrill came over me during a visit to the Wolf Sanctuary near Lititz in Lancaster County in 2018. Although the wolf packs there were safely secured in well-kept fenced pens it was still unnerving when they began to howl, soon becoming a pack in full cry. Their unearthly chorus seemed to come from all sides, and it reverberated throughout the surrounding forest, raising the hairs on the back of my neck even though I knew the wolves could not harm us.

I can also state that after fifty-plus years my original thought, that many if not all of these tales must have some basis in fact, has been strengthened, even though the stories sound to most people like nothing more than tall tales, products from the imaginations of gifted storytellers. It's a conclusion I can defend based on the results of my attempts to explore the historical context behind each tale in order to decide whether or not it contains any kernels of truth within.

It's also a conclusion that was eventually reached even by eminent scholars in the field such as Richard Dorson, who, writing in a 1972 article titled "American Folklore and the Historian," stated "Oral traditions may well exasperate the historian of a literate, or at least print-glutted society, with their quick-silver quality and chronological slipperiness. But they can be trapped, and they offer the chief available records for the beliefs and concerns and memories of large groups of obscured Americans. The historian can find history alive in the field as well as entombed in the library."

To conclude, I'd like to once again thank my son James for the illustrations which appear in this volume; his talent continues to grow over the years. Finally, I'd also like to thank those who continue to write or phone me with book orders or with a tale they think may be of interest. Such material is always a delight to receive, and I invite my readers to continue that practice by calling me at 814-360-4401, emailing me at jandhfra2@yahoo.com, logging on to my website at www.pafiresidetales.com, or sending me a letter at my new address since the death of my wife: 100 Hawknest Way Graystone Court Villas–Apt. 135, Bellefonte PA 16823. I look forward to hearing from you.

—JRF

AUTHOR'S NOTE

The preceding paragraphs are what appeared in previous editions of this volume, and the same chapters that appear in this edition are the same ones that were included in all previous ones. There are also additions to the original chapters. These extras include interesting details that were discovered after the last edition was published and which I felt needed to be added to the chapters in order to enhance their quality.

This new Sunbury Press edition also has many new photos not included in previous editions, but which add a whole new level of interest to the original tales. I hope these enhancements add to the reader's enjoyment. Sunbury Press editions of all my *Pennsylvania Fireside Tales* volumes, and all of my new series titled *Pennsylvania Mountain Landmarks* can be ordered through my publisher (www.SunburyPress.com). Requests to invite me as a speaker at any event can be requested through my publisher also.

—JRF

decency of these characters shine through, reminding us of the enduring power of simple virtues.

In a world that often seems to have lost its sense of wonder, *Pennsylvania Fireside Tales Volume II* is a refreshing reminder of the magic that still exists in the stories passed down through generations. Frazier's collection not only entertains but also rekindles a sense of wonder, bringing these timeless tales vividly to life.

CHAPTER I

GOD'S WARRIORS

What gives a person the strength to go into war? Is it a sense of duty fired by patriotism; or is it a feeling that an injustice needs to be corrected? Fiery speeches and inflammatory writings are the catalysts that decide the issue for some men, but there are others who seem to have an inborn sense of duty that pulls them into the awful chaos of battle. There are many shining examples of unsung heroes like this, but anyone looking for one of them in Pennsylvania need search no further than Jacob Karstetter of Sugar Valley in Clinton County.

Born in 1806, "Jake" Karstetter was the son of one of the first settlers in the pretty little valley that was named for the abundance of sugar maple trees that once could be found here. Although he grew up with the sturdy descendants of other Sugar Valley pioneers, Jake was a "peculiar case." Blessed with exceptional physical strength and an ability to come out the winner in almost any fight in which he participated, it was said Jake "was never willing to stand back," he was also a "splendid" shot.[1]

The sharpshooter was indeed so good with his trusty rifle that it was said that when he took aim he was "dead sure for the bull's eye" every time. Discouraged by his accuracy, Jake's opponents complained long and loudly enough that eventually he was not allowed to participate in the local shooting matches held throughout the region. However, when the Civil War broke out in '61, Jake was determined that his skill with rifle and ball would no longer be denied.

---

1. John Blair Linn, *History of Centre and Clinton Counties*, 613, quoting *the Clinton County Democrat*, January 2, 1873.

Exactly what inspired the Sugar Valley farmer to enlist in the Union army is not recorded, but whatever the motivation, he was "eager for the fray." However, Jake was fifty-four years old at the time and was told by an enlistment officer that he was too old to be mustered in. Unable to change the army's mind, the determined patriot decided to try another approach, even if it meant stretching the truth a bit.

So, sometime later Jake went to another enlistment office and there reported his age as forty-four. That was good enough for the recruiting officer in charge, and so Jake went off to war with the Seventh Pennsylvania, only to end up in the notorious Libby prison near Richmond, Virginia.

After spending an extended period in that Confederate prison pen, the fifty-six-year-old Karstetter returned home and settled down to a peaceful life as a farmer. However, it wasn't long before he got the urge to "join the fray" once more. Realizing he would be refused because of age again, Jake contacted Andrew Gregg Curtin, Pennsylvania's famous war governor, to plead his case.

Curtin directed the feisty farmer to a surgeon who refused him anyway. However, Jake found out "on the sly" that if he paid two hundred and sixty dollars he could be "put through." Not to be denied, the "stout and rugged" patriot paid two hundred dollars to become a soldier, at a time when others were paying even more than that to stay out of the army.

Jacob Karstetter's war record was even more amazing than his fight to go to war in the first place. He fought in over twenty battles, serving part of that time as a sharpshooter. Officers found it hard to keep the independent marksman interested in company duty, and so sometimes allowed him to "go off now and then to have a few shots all to himself." However, one of John S. Mosby's Rebel sharpshooters returned the favor one night when Jake was on picket duty. The Confederate's shot was a near miss, cleanly taking off two of the Federal picket's fingers.[2]

Jake survived the war, spending the rest of his days back in Sugar Valley, but whether he mellowed or not in his old age is open to question. Sometimes old soldiers don't fade away quietly, and if Jake Karstetter was as cantankerous as another Civil War vet from the same valley, he would not have gone out without a fight.

---

2. Ibid.

The older residents of Sugar Valley still remember some of the veterans of the Civil War—elderly men who were still alive when these residents, now elderly themselves, were young boys. A conversation with one of these folks provides a free ticket for a pleasurable journey into the past, and trips such as this are one of the fringe benefits of collecting the old-time tales: interesting anecdotes that reveal the human-interest side of the olden times.

You never know when such memories are going to surface, but on a pleasant summer afternoon while sitting on a front porch in Loganton, a Sugar Valley octogenarian recalled one such episode to several engrossed listeners. We listened intently as the story was told, accompanied now and then by the clatter of horses' hooves as Amish buggies passed by on the main street below.

"Henry Wren was a character," said the old farmer. "Hen," we were told, was highly decorated for bravery in the Civil War, and, when he got older, he wanted to get a government pension for his services. Grover Cleveland was president at the time the vet applied for his stipend, and Wren didn't anticipate any problems. He was one of the most decorated Civil War vets in Sugar Valley, and a pension for such a hero would surely be readily approved. However, due to some bureaucratic error or because of faulty records, his request was denied.

The denial infuriated the old soldier. In a fit of anger, he wrote a letter to the president's wife, or at least that's what the oral history relates. If such an epistle was mailed and received, Mrs. Cleveland must have been surprised when she read it. The complaint itself would not have offended her, but the ending sentences contained language that would certainly have shocked her tender Victorian sensibilities, or those of any other member of the Victorian age's "fairer sex."

Wren, it is said, ended his note with the statement that "he could kiss his ass if the old man [President Cleveland] didn't want to give him a pension." The valley folktales don't go on to state whether Henry Wren ever got his pension or not.[3]

How Henry Wren, Jake Karstetter, or anyone else, could so whole-heartedly throw themselves into the dangers of war is hard for most people to comprehend, and it's even harder for many to understand why any man of

---

3. George Tibbens (born 1913), recorded July 10, 1999.

the cloth would voluntarily elect to participate in an activity once described by Union General William T. Sherman as "hell." However, throughout history religious leaders have struggled with ways to reconcile their religious beliefs and their convictions, with many concluding that they too needed to "join the fray," just like the old soldier from Sugar Valley.

Here in Pennsylvania, there are several notable instances of clerics that seem to have made exceptional contributions as soldiers. Their stories can be found in history books, and a few of these are worth mentioning. However, it will be seen that missing from all these historical examples is a minister of the Civil War era. It's hard to believe that no outstanding cleric-turned-soldier surfaced during that period of exceptional sacrifice, but if there was such a man, historical records seem to have passed him by. Local legend, on the other hand, indicates otherwise, and it's this man's story that should finally be told.

Anyone who remembers their Pennsylvania history or who has read the previous volumes in the *Pennsylvania Fireside Tales* series will recall the many terrible episodes of warfare that echoed and rumbled over Pennsylvania's hills during its first two hundred years of colonial occupation. From the time it was founded in 1681 until the Civil War dyed its soil with blood in the 1860s, Pennsylvania saw its share of conflict.

No one living on Pennsylvania's frontier during the first half of the eighteenth century could have anticipated the terrible and tragic episodes that would occur during the French and Indian Wars of the 1750s. Perhaps that's why, when the war clouds came, every able-bodied frontiersman, including some "sky pilots," as ministers were called in a much later age, became soldiers. Events were too threatening, too horrible, for anyone except the most ardent pacifist to consider other options, including Presbyterian minister John Steel.

Steel's first church was located along the west branch of Conococheague Creek, probably somewhere in present-day Franklin County, about 1755. At that time the chapel was surrounded by a stockade, due to the many incursions of war parties into the region, and Reverend Steel organized a company of riflemen to serve as a defensive unit. Most of the Scotch-Irishmen in the regiment were Steel's parishioners. They not only respected him as the leader of their church but also were as determined as he was to defend the homes and farms they had bought with their sweat and tears, so it seemed natural to elect him as their Captain.

Despite the dangers of the times, Reverend Steel faithfully conducted church services every Sunday, but as a matter of prudent caution the minister and most of the men in the congregation always had their trusty flintlocks and a supply of musket balls by their sides. And so it was that Reverend Steel's little church in the wildwood became known to history as Fort Steel.

Several years later Reverend Steel was even more active in the protection of the frontier, being placed in charge of Fort Allison, near Carlisle. Here, it is said, the parishioners also carried their muskets to church, and minister Steel would bring his, hanging it and his hat on wall pegs behind the pulpit.

One Sunday in the middle of a service, a messenger rushed in with the news that Indians had just murdered the Walker family at nearby Rankin's Mill. Services were quickly ended, and with the parson leading the way, the men in the congregation "went in pursuit of the murderers."[4]

The end of the French and Indian wars of the 1750s brought only momentary peace to the Pennsylvania hills. Ten years later the tribes of the Ohio and Allegheny valleys, led by the great Ottawa chieftain Pontiac, made a determined attempt to sweep colonial frontiersmen from aborigine lands. Once more the pioneers of Pennsylvania heard the war whoop and the scalp halloo, and defense was again the watchword of the times.

Among the determined white defenders of the pioneer settlements during the stirring years of Pontiac's War was Presbyterian minister John Elder of Paxtang, present-day Dauphin County. Here, in the shadows of the Blue Mountains, the Scotch-Irish settlers had no faith that the peace-loving Quakers in Philadelphia would provide money or troops for the defense of what, in those days, was the western frontier. Provisions for dealing with savage marauders would have to be made by the frontiersmen themselves, and so every man once again became a soldier, including Reverend Elder.

Apparently being a man of action, John Elder recruited men from his congregation and formed a company of mounted rangers whose mission was to protect the Paxton settlements from savage raiders. Although they should be given credit for the lives they saved, the "Paxton Boys" are best

---

4. Thomas L. Montgomery, ed., *Frontier Forts of Pennsylvania, Volume 1*, 553.

remembered for their slaughter of innocent Conestogas at the Lancaster County jail in 1763. It was a black mark which will eternally besmirch the names of the Paxtang rangers, but John Elder's is not included in that infamous list.

Elder tried to convince his rangers not to go; they couldn't, he insisted, tell the guilty from the innocent, but when the men threatened to shoot his favorite horse, the "fighting parson of Paxtang," as he became known, had to step aside.[5] Later he might have had second thoughts about his involvement in matters of warfare when he heard about the Conestoga children, women, and old men the rangers indiscriminately massacred that day.

It would appear that Presbyterians had a monopoly on fighting parsons during the 1750s and 1760s in Pennsylvania, but in the decade after Pontiac's War there was a Lancaster County Presbyterian cleric who had a different outlook than John Elder or John Steel.

Preserved in the annals of the Donegal Presbyterian Church in Lancaster County is the story of the "Witness Tree," which stood in front of the sanctuary until about fifty years ago, when blight and old age finally claimed it. It was around this giant oak, so says the old legend which clings to the ancient church to this day, that the entire congregation formed a circle in June of 1777, and while holding hands, pledged their fidelity to the Revolution and to the Colonial government.

Their minister, however, was not amused, steadfastly proclaiming that his sympathies rested with King George rather than with the colonists. Although the minister's political opinions were tolerated, they were definitely not accepted. Tensions boiled over one Sunday morning, sometime after the congregation's declaration of support for the Revolution, when the Tory pastor was in the middle of the church service. Suddenly his sermon was interrupted by a horseman who had traveled at break-neck speed to announce that General Washington needed men to help defend Philadelphia from the British.

Reverend McFarquhar, still maintaining his allegiance to the king, spoke out against the request, whereupon his congregation dragged the helpless cleric out to the witness tree and made him "raise his hat in allegiance to the Revolution."[6]

---

5. C. Hale Sipe, *The Indian Wars of Pennsylvania*, 463–66.

6. Grant N. Sassaman, ed., *Pennsylvania, A Guide to the Keystone State*, 443; William H. Egle, *History of Pennsylvania*, 849.

The memory of the Donegal church's Tory minister has almost been swept into the dustbins of history over the years, and that seems a proper fate when the story of another minister of that same period is recalled.

John Peter Gabriel Muhlenberg was not a typical Pennsylvania Dutchman. Born in 1746 to German immigrants in Eastern Pennsylvania, Muhlenberg was a natural born leader of men. However, this grandson of the great Indian agent Conrad Weiser chose to heed the call of the church, and so became a Lutheran minister. His first parish was in the Shenandoah Valley of Virginia where his leadership qualities were recognized by colonial authorities.

Then, in 1776, the young minister was asked by these same authorities to raise a regiment of soldiers which would become part of Washington's army. Muhlenberg kept his assignment a secret until the next Sunday's church service when he wore a full Continental officer's uniform underneath his ministerial robes.

Statue of John Peter Muhlenberg (with the cape that hid the uniform). In the Capitol Building's National Statuary Hall, Washington, DC.

Using Ecclesiastes III as his text, the thirty-year-old cleric inspired his congregation with a rousing sermon, concluding with the famous lines: "For everything its season, and for every activity under heaven its time: a time to be born and a time to die; a time for war and a time for peace." Then, pausing for effect, the young officer pulled open his robe, revealing his officer's uniform, and thundered, "There is a time to pray and a time to fight; now is the time to fight!"

History records that hundreds of stalwart men joined Muhlenberg's regiment; and notes that the cleric-turned-soldier was so effective in his military role that he ended that career as a major general. He also came out of the war with a nickname that revealed the respect enemy soldiers had for

Portrait of General Peter Muhlenberg or "Teufil Piet"
(Devil Pete) to the British soldier!

their crafty adversary. Impressed by his military prowess, the king's Hessian troops called the general *Teufel Piet*. It meant "Devil Pete."[7]

Twenty more years passed after the end of the Revolutionary War before war clouds once again darkened the war-torn hills of the Keystone State. The War of 1812, like its predecessors, produced heroes worthy of mention in any histories of the times, and among those heroes was Reverend William Johnston of Dunlap's Creek in Fayette County.

Convinced that the people of Uniontown and surrounding communities were not behind the war as much as they should be, the fiery cleric marched into the Uniontown courthouse one day in 1814 and preached a hellfire-and-damnation sermon as to why the war effort should be supported.

Using Jeremiah 48, verse 10, as his text (Cursed be he that keepeth back his sword from blood), Johnston inspired one hundred and eighteen men to enlist on the spot. However, the young minister had also managed to fire up the anti-war groups in the town, who thereafter called him the "Bloody Parson." It was a name that stuck with him until the day he died.[8]

---

7. C. Hale Sipe, *The Indian Chiefs of Pennsylvania*, 126–27.
8. George Swetnam, *Pittsylvania Country*, 124.

Painting of a bearded Conrad Weiser accepting a wampum belt from chief
Shikellamy. Guides at the Weiser Homestead relate the interesting story
that Shikellamy once asked Conrad Weiser to shave off his beard because it
was frightening Indiam children! Painted from memory by Moravian John
Valentine Haidt, the likenesses are not considered accurate since the artist never
met any of the men on the painting, including Count Nikolaus Zinzendorf on
the left. Weiser's daughter Maria married Henry Muhlenberg, and their son
John Peter Muhlenberg (Teufil Piet of Revolutionary War fame) was Conrad
Weiser's grandson.

After the War of 1812, the gods of strife were satisfied for almost fifty
more years until they needed to see blood spilled upon Pennsylvania's soil
once again. This time it was the Civil War that those gods would send
down upon the state's peaceful hills and valleys, and in some respects, it
was the worst war of all in terms of the human toll it exacted. Men from all
walks of life were drawn into and destroyed by the great conflict, including
ministers of many different denominations.

However, none of these clerics seem to stand out in history like a Captain John Steel, and none of them have left their marks on the historical
record like the "Fighting Parson of Paxtang," *Teufel Piet* Muhlenberg, or
the "Bloody Parson" of Uniontown. Consequently, it would seem that the
clergy of that era were less apt to pick up the sword than any of their

predecessors, but legends and folktales, at least in one case, paint a different picture in that regard.

The story of Lewis Edmunds, minister of a Reformed church in the small Centre County town of Aaronsburg during the Civil War, has been forgotten by the present generation. It was never a tale that was widely heard, and even thirty years ago there were few residents of the area who could still remember it.

And one of the last men, if not the very last one, who could recall the episode died in the 1980s. He had heard about it when he was just a boy, and so even though the exact details were sketchy, the salient points were well-remembered and form an intriguing addition to the legendary annals of the Civil War.

Not everyone north of the Mason-Dixon Line was a supporter of Mr. Lincoln's war. Some of these more determined secessionists, known as "copperheads" or "seceshs" by northern sympathizers, formed secret organizations to undermine the federal war effort in any way they could, including using intimidation if they thought it would work.

It is remembered by some that an organization called the Knights of the Golden Circle used such tactics, and their "coffin notices" added yet another bitter ingredient to the bubbling cauldron that had boiled over and drenched the land with the terrible stench of war.

Whenever the Knights in Columbia County found out that a young man there was thinking of enlisting as an officer in the Union army, they would attempt to discourage him by sending him an empty coffin with a malicious message inside. The same organization was also active south of Nittany Mountain in John Penn's Valley of Centre County.

There were many young Penns Valley men who marched off to war and gave the folks at home reasons to be proud, but the area also had nests of Copperheads who helped other recruits avoid service altogether. In the mountains south of Penns View, near the little village of Coburn, it is said that there was a "deserters' camp" where a draftee would be sent to "lay low" until the authorities gave up looking for him. At one time there were as many as thirty-four deserters in the camp, and "a large group of citizens would provide them with clothes, food, and ammunition."[9]

---

9. Blaine Malone (born 1903), *History of Coburn* (privately published manuscript). Interviewed October 23, 1980, and April 21, 1981.

Anti-war sentiment ran high at times in other valley communities too, culminating in one case with an effigy burning by war protestors. In Haines Township there were anti-war sentiments as well, with one draft evader shooting himself in the toe to avoid service, and another hiding in a cave until the end of the war. These were individual acts, but many of Aaronsburg's citizens were in sympathy, especially those who were members of Lewis Edmunds' congregation.

Edmunds' opinions on the war were no secret. He was a supporter of the Union's conflict with the south, but he was in a position much like that of the notorious McFarquhar of Donegal Church during the

Reverend (and Lieutenant) Lewis C. Edmunds, 148th Pennsylvania Vols. (from Muffley's History of the 148th).

Revolution. Members of Edmunds' church were anti-war men, and they had made it clear to him that if he enlisted, they would fire him.

Undaunted, and perhaps familiar with the story of how Peter Muhlenberg surprised his congregation by wearing a uniform under his clerical robes, Edmunds, according to local legend, did the same thing. Wearing the blue uniform of a Union officer under his black gown, the brave young minister walked into the church and conducted the service as usual. Then in the middle of his sermon, he pulled open his robe and announced he was "going off to war."[10]

Valley folktales say that Lewis Edmunds survived the war and came back to live in a house in High Valley, above Coburn. Here, below the lofty peaks of the White Mountains, Edmunds spent his final years, passing away peacefully and gradually fading out of peoples' memories. A family of mountain folks moved into the vacant house shortly after the old soldier's death, but eventually they began to tell their neighbors that they couldn't sleep at night.

Unnatural sounds kept them awake, they said. The loudest noises reminded them of chains rattling, but that cacophony would always die

---

10. Paul Bartges, interviewed August 28, 1972; Myrtle Magargel, "The Rebellion in the North," *Centre Daily Times*, Bellefonte, PA, February 23–26, 1937.

Entrance gate to Paxton Church Cemetery. (Burial place of Rev. John Elder, the
"Fighting Parson of Paxtang.")

Pennsylvania Historical marker at Paxton Church. (Dauphin County)

down. It was the following, less strident sound, one that was almost as soft as a whisper, that proved to be the most unnerving to the isolated mountaineers.

They all knew the story of Lewis Edmunds and how he hid his army uniform under his ministerial robe, and the softer noise they heard at night sounded to them just like a heavy garment being dragged over the floors of the house. Unable to stand the nocturnal doings any longer, the hill hawks decided to leave, and they probably moved out on an April Fool's Day, the typical day for flittings in the Pennsylvania Dutch regions.[11]

The Edmunds place was occupied by a series of other families over the years, but whether it was just too isolated, or whether it was too haunted, eventually no one wanted to live there, and the old place gradually fell into disrepair. Nonetheless, it did not lose its appeal to humans entirely.

As the deserted homestead became more and more haunted-looking, people began to recall the stories of the noises that drove residents away, and local teenagers were attracted to the house, seeing it as a place where they could test their mettle by spending a night inside.

Eventually, as nothing out of the ordinary was ever heard by any of them, they, too, left the place to its ghosts. It was the final nail in Lewis Edmunds' coffin. His story and his name were forgotten by all but a few of those teenagers, one of whom told the story to me in 1972 when he was an old man.

NOTES:

Records from the German Reformed Church in Aaronsburg list the ministers who served that charge, starting in 1852. Included in that roll is the name L. C. Edmunds.

In the muster roll of the 148th Pennsylvania Volunteers for August 28, 1862, is the name of second lieutenant Lewis C. Edmunds of Haines Township, Centre County.[12] Edmunds couldn't have joined a better squad. General James Beaver's regiment was a well-trained and well-disciplined fighting unit, qualities that would serve them well during later engagements at places like Cold Harbor, Hatcher's Run, and Chancellorsville.

---

11. Hannah Barnhart (born 1823), from a manuscript written for her descendants in 1898, (copy given to the author by Mr. Ellis Hall of Unionville, PA, August 1999).

12. John Blair Linn, *History of Centre and Clinton Counties*, 127, 158.

John Elder's Tombstone with an inscription that reads: "The body of the late Rev. John Elder lies interred under this slab. He departed this life July 17th, 1792."

However, one other quality distinguished "Jimmy" Beaver's outfit from others, and that was the General's habit of leading his men in prayer every day. It was a practice that must have delighted Lewis Edmunds, and it also certainly impressed other Federal troops, who referred to the 148th as "the praying regiment."[13]

An account of the day Lewis Edmunds wore his uniform to church is preserved in Muffly's *History of the 148th Pennsylvania Volunteers* (see page 618). Here the entire episode about the day he wore his uniform to church is recounted, and it is also recalled how disliked he was for doing so.

He had been forewarned by a committee of churchmen not to enlist, but he did so anyway, and when told to discard his uniform by the same men he said he could not "lay it off," and went off to war. Afterwards one of his parishioners was supposed to have said "*mer sut den Schwartz Republikaner uf der strose um schiese*" (Someone ought to shoot down this black Republican upon our street). Others agreed, saying they wished that the "first bullet of the Rebs would hit Edmonds."

Today it's hard for us to believe how deep-seated and widespread the opposition to the Union cause actually was in that day. However, after the

---

13. John J. Serff, "General, Governor, Judge—James A. Beaver," *Centre County Heritage 1956–1975*, 11.

conflict was over even the staunchest opponents seemed to finally realize that the fighting had been "good for the country and for humanity."

Even a resolution put forth by the vestry of Edmunds' church that decreed he should never be allowed to preach there again was finally rescinded, and the gallant soldier subsequently preached there many times. Nonetheless, it seems apparent that the stories of Peter Muhlenberg and that of Lewis Edmunds became intertwined over the years, making Edmunds that much more of a folk hero.[14]

---

14. J. W. Muffly, *The Story of Our Regiment—A History of the 148th Pennsylvania Volunteers*, 618–19.

CHAPTER II

BIG CATS OF THE
BIG WOODS

Embedded in the county histories of the Keystone State are many exciting accounts of how *Felis cougar*, also variously known across the commonwealth as the puma, cougar, painter, panther, or mountain lion, was sometimes hunted down by determined nimrods. On the other hand, there are just as many accounts of how the wily felines sometimes turned the tables so that the hunters became the hunted. In those cases, the ferocious cats, when viewed by the person being chased, may have indeed looked larger than life.

Fortunately, we have more than just subjective personal narratives to determine the actual size of the mountain lions that roamed the forests of those times. Naturalists and biologists of that era recorded statistics on the panthers that were brought in for the easy bounty money that was offered for the beasts, and those records show that the lions were often as large as our mountaineers claimed.

In his fascinating work entitled *Mammals of Pennsylvania and New Jersey*, published in 1903, naturalist Samuel N. Rhoads states that of all the panthers killed in the United States up to that time, some of the largest "have been killed in Pennsylvania and Louisiana."[1] Historian W. J. McKnight agreed, noting that hunters in Pennsylvania occasionally shot panthers that were "ten feet from nose to tip of tail."[2] Although the average

---

1. Samuel N. Rhoads, *Mammals of Pennsylvania and New Jersey*, 135.
2. W. J. McKnight, *Pioneer Outline History of Northwestern Pennsylvania*, 176–77.

panther was usually somewhat smaller than that, it was still a formidable creature, as can be seen from the historical record.

Captain Joshua Sabin, veteran of the Revolutionary War and a well-known Susquehanna County hunter, settled on a farm in the Hop Bottom country of that county after the conflict with Britain. Here, in what is now Brooklyn Township, he killed, by his own estimate, "five panthers, a number of bears, some seven or eight wolves, and at least two hundred deer" during the four-year period from 1800 to 1803. One of the panthers was shot with a musket, "loaded with eleven buckshot," which Sabin set up near the carcass of a deer that the panther had killed.

The big cat had covered the dead deer with leaves, and the wily hunter knew it would return later that night to feast upon its kill. When it did come back as expected, it triggered Sabin's musket, and every shot found its mark. The large feline, according to Sabin's measurements, "measured nine feet in length from his nose to the end of his tail."[3]

A panther measuring "eight feet and a few inches" was killed by wolf hunter Michael Scheffer in Clearfield County about 1823. One day while out checking his wolf traps, Scheffer came to the trunk of a huge tree that had fallen over into a thicket.

Deciding to use the tree trunk as a pathway through the dense forest glen, the wolf hunter started across. Part way over he looked down and spied the animal looking up at him. The unarmed pioneer managed to retrieve a good sized "war club," got back on the log, and "with well-directed blows knocked the panther's brains out."[4]

In 1857 a panther measuring nine feet two inches, nose tip to tail tip, was shot by a deer hunter in Chapman Township of Clinton County. The man who measured this fallen monarch of the forest was amazed, noting that, had he not seen it for himself, he would never have believed "so formidable an animal inhabited our woods."[5]

Many other examples like this could be noted here, but from those already given, it's not hard to imagine the fear these mighty beasts must have engendered in the minds of the mountain folks that were their neighbors. However, it wasn't just the accounts of their size that made the big cats seem so formidable.

---

3. Emily C. Blackman, *History of Susquehanna County, Pennsylvania*, 119.
4. Lewis Cass Aldrich, *History of Clearfield County, Pennsylvania*, 459.
5. John Blair Linn, *History of Centre and Clinton Counties, Pennsylvania*, 585.

There were also tales of panthers attacking humans, which were regarded as exaggerations by experienced mountain men like Clinton County pioneer hunter Philip Tome, who claimed such stories were "undoubtedly without foundation."[6] No doubt attacks were rare in Tome's time, the late 1700s when there were fewer people encroaching upon the natural habitat of the mountain lion, but as more people settled in the virgin forests of the interior, such encounters would become more commonplace.

The Pennsylvania panthers proved to be a stubborn lot, clinging to their old haunts in the mountains and refusing to be dislodged without a fight. Many were the nights that the early settlers heard the defiant sound of "the painter's cry" from the top of the ridges towering over their humble cabins. And it is from these early times, and even into the first decades of the 1900s, that accounts of people being confronted by the big cats have come down to us.

They have been recorded in both history books, and also in non-recorded fast-disappearing oral traditions. It is those oral traditions that have been passed on through descendants of the hardy mountaineers who lived in those thrilling times. First from children, then to grandchildren, and on to great grandchildren, and so on.

Turning first to the historical records, there is an account in Miss Blackman's *History of Susquehanna County* about a panther attacking Mrs. Edmund Stone of Bridgewater Township about 1811. Mrs. Stone had attended a meeting at the "South school-house" and was returning home on horseback, carrying her child in her arms. As she passed through a dark woods, a panther that was concealed alongside the trail made a mighty leap in an attempt to spring upon the hapless woman and her baby. Fortunately for the mother and infant the cat must have been an old one or young and inexperienced, because it missed its aim and "passed over the horse's head."[7]

Two Lackawanna County men could also thank their lucky stars one frosty moonlit night in the fall of 1837 when they were returning home from a country tavern in Wayne County. Harry Hollister and a friend were riding in a horse and buggy on what was then called the old Connecticut road, and around midnight they passed by a vast swampland the early

6. Philip Tome, *Pioneer Life or Thirty Years a Hunter*, 111.
7. Emily C. Blackman, *History of Susquehanna County, Pennsylvania*, 305.

settlers had named the Shades of Death, due to its bleak and foreboding aspects.

Somewhere in this desolate and gloomy stretch the chilling screams of a panther arose from a dense thicket of alder bushes, hemlocks, and mountain laurel alongside the road. The cries were loud enough to startle the most stout-hearted mountaineer, but when the enormous beast sprang onto the road behind them, he was so close that the men could hear the dry limbs crack as he emerged from his hiding place.

The eerie silence of the night was temporarily interrupted by the screams of the pursuing beast, the quickening beat of the horse's hooves on the frozen highway, and the rumble of the wagon's wheels as they clattered over the many stones in the road. For eight miles the tawny panther bounded after the speeding buggy, always managing to remain within a stone's throw of the frightened horse and men.

The horse began to tire as evanescent clouds of vapor, no doubt looking like puffs of smoke as they formed in the cold moonlit night, came more rapidly from its mouth and nostrils. Finally, the panther tired also, and the horse was able to out-distance it, allowing the men to reach the relative safety of the spot known as Little Meadows.

It was an unforgettable experience, and the screams of the beast left a permanent impression on the minds of the two travelers. The sounds were so "distinct and appalling," they noted, that they had no further desire to ever encounter another panther.[8]

Up in Elk County, about 1855, a young man named Ben McClelland had a panther scare that was just as unnerving as that of the two Lackawanna County lads almost twenty years earlier. Ben worked for Sheriff Healey during the winter of 1855–56, and the sheriff sent the young teamster on an errand to Warren, Warren County, with a sled and two horses.

The sleigh ride to Warren was uneventful, and his business there was completed quickly enough so that on his trip back young McClelland expected to make it as far as Highland in Elk County before nightfall. Here he would spend the night, get an early start the next morning, and make it home the same day.

The trip back took a little longer than Ben had hoped, and the curtains of night seemed to be closing quickly. A few miles north of Highland, at

---

8. H. Hollister, *History of the Lackawanna Valley*, 291.

a lonely place that had been aptly named Panther Hollow after the beasts that often made it their home, the darkness became complete. Then the horses spooked. Something alongside the road scared them, and they snorted in fear, galloping away at an uncontrollable pace. Turning around, McClelland was shocked to see a panther bounding after him.

Seemingly afraid of the sled, the panther avoided the road, but this slowed it down as it had to plow through the deep snow along the side. It was still a neck-to-neck race to Highland, and although Ben was a hunter, he had no gun with him that night. Finally, the cheerful lights in the Townley farmhouse could be seen, and when the Townley's cleared fields were reached the panther gave up the chase.

By this time the runaway horses were spent and lathered, and Ben, it was said, was almost dead from fright. Early the next morning, the panther, who had been the hunter the previous night, fell victim to a party of local farmers who tracked the big brute and found it near the hollow. Here they killed it, but the story of the big cat's attack and its demise must have only strengthened the reputation of the "Panther Hollow" as a place to avoid at night.[9]

Another wintertime panther scare occurred in Clearfield County about 1903–1904 when a mother and her daughter were pursued by a big cat while on a neighborly mission. Fifty-five years later the daughter remembered the event in a letter to a local hunter, who sent me a copy some twenty years after that:

> When I was a little girl of three or four, my parents lived in Morgan Run, on a place called the old Coffee Place [wrote Rosie Bailor in 1959]. My daddy, Ed Lindenmuth, was the blacksmith at the mines, and my mother was Christ Pool's daughter. He was an old-time lumberman and helped cut a lot of the virgin timber in Elk and Cameron Counties.
>
> One winter my dad butchered a big hog, and my mother did up some of the meat and put it in a basket. She dressed me up good and warm, put me on a sled, and gave me the basket to hold. She had friends at Sanbourne and intended to give them some of our fresh meat. When she put me on the sled, she put

9. W. J. McKnight, *Pioneer Outline History of Northwestern Pennsylvania*, 517.

me facing back so the wind wouldn't blow in my face while she hauled me. William Brouse lived about halfway to Sanbourne, and on the other side of the road was woods.

A big cat followed us. He went back and forth across the road, and when his head was on one side his tail reached clear across to the other. My mom told me the cat wanted our basket of meat and told me to kick it out of the sled for the cat. I cried and fought, as I didn't want to give our meat to the cat. At last she told me that if I didn't give the cat the meat it would eat me. It had slapped at me with its big foot and hissed.

When at last I gave the cat the meat, it purred like a big house cat, but much louder and coarser. Since I've grown up, I know now that the big cat was a panther, and that my mother was very much afraid of it. Mother told me that she was afraid every minute it would decide to tackle us. I'm glad now it took the meat instead of mom or me![10]

Rosie Bailor would go on to become a well-respected hunting guide in the big-woods country of Clearfield and Elk Counties that she loved so much, and she would see more panthers in her interesting career, recording each encounter in her "personal experience book of contact with animals."

However, even though on several occasions she got close enough to a big cat "to feel its hot breath in my face," Rosie never killed a panther. Either the clever beasts were too quick and got away before she could shoot them, or she was never armed when they did cross her path, but the hide of a Pennsylvania lion never adorned Rosie's hunting lodge on Sander's Run.

The reason being, as most hunters of the first half of the twentieth century would likely have professed, that a trophy like a panther's hide was hard to come by at that late date. On the other hand, there were probably other nimrods around that time that might have expressed a different opinion.

The more superstitious outdoorsmen among them might have recalled the panther over in Lycoming County that killed a doctor near English Center around 1896 (which is the date on the monument that stands along

---

10. Harris Breth, letter from Rosie Bailor, dated April 2, 1959.

The Reinwald Monument. English Center Bed and Breakfast is in the background; lost to fire several years ago. (Photo taken near English Center, Lycoming County, in 2018.)

the roadside near English Center today—see the author's *Pennsylvania Fireside Tales Volume III*. Naturalist Rhoads, in his *Mammals of Pennsylvania and New Jersey*, says the date was about 1840.)

The incident in question involved a young country doctor named Frederick Reinwald, who practiced in Liberty Corners, Tioga County. One winter day the doctor received a message that he was urgently needed in English Center, Lycoming County. The distance being only about five miles, Reinwald did not hesitate.

Picking up his medicine bag and a double-barreled rifle for protection, the good doctor mounted his horse and set off for English Center. As the hours passed and the last rays of daylight finally faded into the lead-gray skies of winter, people in Liberty Corners became concerned. The doctor had not returned when expected, and heavy snow had begun to fall.

A search party finally went out to look for the missing medical man, but the deep drifts made the task a long and difficult one. Two weeks later his body was found beside a large butternut tree, where, it was evident, he had been attacked and killed by a panther. The doctor apparently hadn't

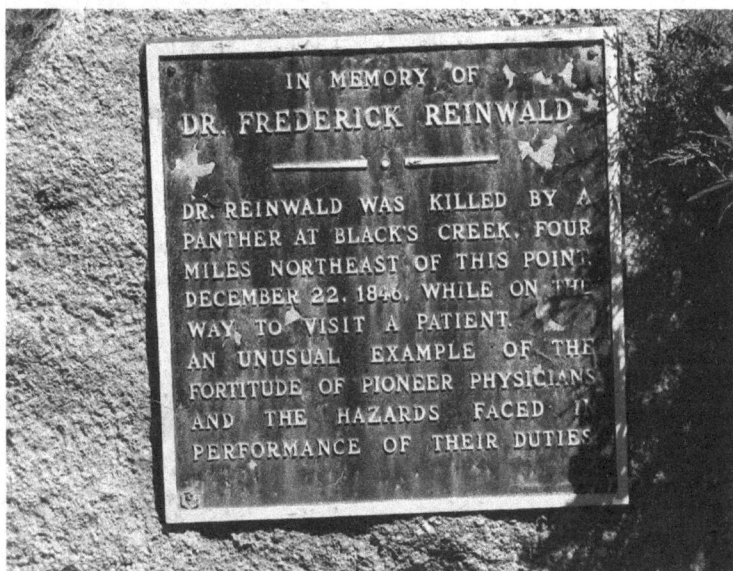

The Plaque on the Reinwald Monument. (The inscription on the plaque commemorates the doctor who lost his life to a panther while doing his medical duties.

gone out without a fight, as one barrel of his gun had been discharged. He had also attempted to fire the second barrel, but it had misfired.

It was concluded by the searchers that the doctor had seen the panther on an overhanging limb of the big butternut and had shot it. To them it seemed obvious that the wounded panther, in a pain-induced rage, then "sprang from the limb upon the unfortunate man."[11]

Superstition still ruled the minds of many of the Pennsylvania Dutchman in this section of the mountains known as the Block-House Country in those times. The misguided beliefs and legends of the original German pioneers who had built the log block-house as a protection from aboriginal war parties would prove almost as hard to down as the Indians had been. For that reason, it would appear that the men who found Doc Reinwald's body were convinced that there just was something quite strange about the whole affair.

It would not have taken much of a marksman to kill such a large and well-exposed animal with one shot at such a close range, yet the doctor had failed to do so; and when he attempted to shoot again, his gun misfired.

---

11. Samuel N. Rhoads, *Mammals of Pennsylvania and New Jersey*, 130.

Chased by a mountain lion while sleighing through the woods. Depiction of a Clearfield County panther attack as recalled by Rosie Bailor. (Drawing by James J. Frazier.)

This was a scenario all too familiar to some of the men. Witches could bewitch animals so they could not be shot, or these hexes could even "take the fire" from a man's gun, so as to render it harmless. Believing whole-heartedly in these possibilities, Reinwald's friends readily concluded this must have been the reason that lead to his death.

The following winter two deer hunters spotted panther tracks in the mountains above Liberty Corners. Jacob Sechrist and Mr. Messner had known Frederick Reinwald and had considered him a friend. It was, they felt, their duty to avenge the doctor's death in any way they could, and so they talked about what to do next. Agreeing that the panther was probably under the spell of a witch, the two hunters returned home to make the necessary preparations for a protracted hunt.

The next morning, they returned to the spot where they had found the panther's tracks. With them they had provisions to last for several days, and each man also carried a "witch-proof" rifle, loaded with a musket ball made of pure silver, which, they believed, was the only sure remedy to counteract any spell a witch had placed upon an animal.

For three days and nights the determined hunters trailed the panther, sleeping on snow-covered ground when night came. On the fourth day they caught up to the big cat in Sullivan County. There, east of Loyalsock Creek, on the mountain near Hillsgrove, they were able to get a clear shot at the elusive lion. When they skinned it, they found a grisly reminder of their friend. In the shoulder of the beast was a rifle ball, which, they concluded, was probably Doctor Reinwald's.[12]

History doesn't go on to say what the men did with the dead panther, but they were probably satisfied to tell all the doctor's friends that they had avenged his death, despite the best efforts of a witch to prevent them from doing so, and that there was now one less big cat roaming the big woods of northern Pennsylvania.

---

12. Ibid.

CHAPTER III

THE BEAVER DAM WITCH

At the foot of the eastern terminus of Egg Hill in Gregg Township, Centre County, where the cool waters of Sinking Creek flow into those of Penn's Creek, there are many ideal locations for water-powered mills. Shrewd early settlers in the area were quick to realize the business opportunities the waters afforded, and so here, in the shadow of Egg Hill, many mills were eventually erected, including a sawmill and a grist mill which were built by 1793.

It was the prevalence of these mills, along with the discovery of many natural springs in the area, that suggested the name for the town which grew up at this site. Today there are no mills left in the tiny hamlet of Spring Mills, but its name reminds us of the time when there were many, thereby serving as a link to the past.

It's the history behind the names, the human-interest side of that history in particular, that makes the study of place names so interesting. In the case of the mountain above Spring Mills, for example, elderly locals claimed that the first German settlers here named the little ridge *Oie Holle*, which, when translated into English, means Egg Hill. Lifelong valley resident Clarence Musser, born in 1884, told me in 1971 that the original settlers here came up with that name because they found so many wild turkey nests filled with eggs all over the mountain; a fact not well-known today.

That's the case with many of the names of creeks, valleys, mountains, and small towns in Pennsylvania. The origins of their quaint names have almost been forgotten over time; that, in itself, is enough reason to include a chapter on this subject in this volume of the *Pennsylvania Fireside Tales* series (see also the chapter titled "What's in a Name" in the author's *Pennsylvania Fireside Tales Volume VI* for origins of more interesting and unusual Pennsylvania place names). However, the topic is discussed here only as an opportunity to mention the quaint little settlement of Beaver Dam, which lies along the crick road, as locals would say, about two miles southeast of Spring Mills.

Beaver Dam, as might be guessed, was so named because the first settlers in the area found that a colony of beavers had arrived here first. Attracted to the pure deep waters of Penns Creek, the busy little animals constructed a huge dam of mud and branches that must have been quite impressive.

It was at least noteworthy enough that people decided to use the name when referring to the spot, and so the beavers' edifice must have become one of the landmarks people mentioned when attempting to give directions to those unfamiliar to the area. But time and the elements have a way of erasing even the most magnificent natural wonders, and nature didn't hold back when it unleashed its inexorable forces upon the beaver dam.

The Beaver Dam Schoolhouse as it looks today, along Penns Creek, Centre County.

The beavers, for whatever their reason, abandoned their construction project, and eventually it collapsed, or was ripped apart by human hands, all final traces probably washing away in one of the many spring floods that were once so common in the mountains. Nonetheless, the disappearance of this remarkable structure didn't erase its memory from the minds of the local populace, and although it was gone it was not forgotten, the name Beaver Dam still being used as the name for this locale today. And just as the name Spring Mills recalls the mills that once stood there, the name Beaver Dam reminds us of the landmark that once spanned the waters at this spot.

Unless they make a concerted attempt to look for the place, most people today most likely might think that there is no longer anyone living at Beaver Dam, that it is only an abandoned site or ghost town. That would not be true, and there are no ghosts that haunt the immediate area, at least none that I've been told about. However, Beaver Dam did once have its witch, but that's a story that was almost swept away in the currents of time; almost as forgotten as the little hamlet itself.

Along the back road linking the villages of Spring Mills and Coburn in Centre County, and almost completely hidden among the trees that shade the northern edge of Penns Creek, the little cluster of houses that comprises the village of Beaver Dam sits well off the beaten path. It is a place that is easily overlooked by the passing motorist. Although its location accounts for some of this oversight, the scenery here is probably the main reason that the eyes of passersby are diverted in other directions instead of toward the other side of the creek.

Lovers of the quaint corners and by-ways of the Pennsylvania mountains should add this stretch of the Penns Creek Road to their list of trips to take some weekend when wanderlust strikes. The scenery along this little-traveled country highway is beautiful at any time of the year, with either the impressive heights of First Mountain to the south or Egg Hill to the west always within view; but the trip should preferably be taken in the fall after the leaves have taken on their autumn colors.

It is during this season that the senses seem more attuned to the past, and so it is this time of year when thoughts might turn to what life around Beaver Dam must have been like over a hundred years ago. This is especially true for those who appreciate the few remaining relatively unspoiled sections of the state and the legends they still harbor.

For these lovers of quaint and forgotten lore, questions naturally come to mind concerning what human episodes, tales, and legends of the dim past might still be heard here. However, to feel the full effect of this place, and to get a real yearning for its legends, the visit should be made in the month of October; the month of ghosts, goblins, and witches.

By the time the Gay Nineties rolled around, the citizens of Beaver Dam and the surrounding countryside were used to hearing the shriek of the steam engine's whistle and the sounds of boxcars clattering along steel tracks. It had been about twenty years since the Lewisburg, Centre, and Spruce Creek Railroad laid down its rails along Penns Creek in 1877, and by this time the area's residents must have thought they had entered the modern age; that a new order of things had finally arrived, and that old ways were fading rapidly into the past.

Although that may have been true in most respects, there were certain aspects of life that were slow to change, and among those were the ancient superstitions and beliefs that were brought here from the Old Country. And included in these deep-seated beliefs was a strong attachment to ideas concerning witchcraft.

In this respect Beaver Dam was no different than neighboring communities in those days. Each one could lay claim to its share of witches, both good ones, known as *brauchers*, and bad types, often called hexes, and each town had at least one sorcerer or sorceress that seemed to be more infamous than the other local witches. In Beaver Dam's case, there was the hex they called Amanda.

Her last name is no longer remembered, other than the fact that it "was a common name like Smith,"[1] but the people who lived near her all regarded her with some suspicion. Many claimed she was a hex, though none could prove it, but there were ways that could be used to do so—or so claimed the pundits who knew about such matters. One day a group of young ladies, unable to contain their curiosity any longer, decided they would take matters into their own hands.

---

1. Helen Elder (born 1921), recorded June 5, 1998.

A mountain farm family. Taken around 1905, this picture shows the typical lifestyle of families that lived in the hills and mountains of Pennsylvania around the turn of the nineteenth century. The Eberts (John and Julia and their children) lived near the small village of Beaver Dam in Centre County.

Living in, or close to, the little village of Beaver Dam in the last years of the 1890s was a family named Ebert. Julia Dunlap Ebert and her husband John had six sons and six daughters, and the daughters were curious about the neighbor lady who often came to sit and sew with their mother. Amanda and her daughter Mary seemed like normal folks, but Amanda had a darker side, or so claimed the local gossips, and the Ebert sisters, Alice, Julia, Verna, Bertha, Minnie, and Lydia, decided to observe her carefully every time she came for a visit.[2]

A common belief of those times was that a witch would not step over a broom. This idea must have seemed incongruous to some when it was recalled that in addition to boiling cauldrons, black cats, and ancient tomes of malicious incantations, a broom was just as important to practitioners of the black arts as the Bible was to those who used it to counteract a hex's spells. In the witch's case, it was the broom that could sometimes be used

---

2. Ibid.

like a huge magic wand of sorts when conjuring up bad weather, and it was also the broom that afforded her a means of transportation.

Stories of witches riding astride their brooms were favorite tales often heard and often repeated in those days. And even yet today pictures of an old hag flying through the air atop her broomstick are still common decorations that can be seen around Halloween during the witching month of October.

Rather than question the obvious paradox of the broom's utility to the witch on the one hand and her aversion to it on the other, the Ebert sisters decided to check these things out for themselves. After much discussion they finally agreed to put the broom test to good use one day when Amanda and her daughter Mary came to sew.

Sometime after the visitors arrived, the curious Ebert girls took a broom and placed it where Amanda would have to step across it when leaving the house. Undoubtedly the minutes must have seemed like hours as the afternoon passed. As time dragged on the sisters' emotions must have

A witch riding her broomstick. Artist's depiction of how many once thought a witch and her black cat might appear when sailing through the sky in her peaked hat and crossing over the face of a creamy white moon.

swung back and forth between excitement and fear while they waited for their mother's guests to leave, but the time finally came.

"Well, it was towards evening and time to go home," recalled Alice Ebert's daughter, who had heard the tale from her mother.

"And Amanda said to her daughter, 'Come on Mary,' she said, 'we have to get home and take care of supper.'

"And she started to the door and saw the broomstick. And she wouldn't step over; so, they assumed she was a witch!"[3]

The broom episode must have inspired the Ebert sisters to keep an even closer watch on their mysterious neighbor whenever she came to sew. Now even more suspicious and watchful, they, on another occasion, saw her doing something they would later aver was even more damning than her failure to step over a broom.

"My grandmother and them had an out-building where they kept stuff," continued Alice's daughter.

"And she said for one of the kids to go get milk. 'We're out of milk'.

"And Amanda said, 'Oh no you're not!'

"And the kids saw her in the kitchen take a tea towel and knead it like she was milking a cow. And she got milk!

"They went around telling this story to other people, and there was a young lady who decided she would like to be a witch too, if you can do things like that."

The witch-wannabe was serious about pursuing her dreams, and so she contacted Amanda's daughter Mary, asking her to ask her mother what a person who wanted to be a witch had to do to become one.

"The girl told her mother," continued our story-teller, "and Amanda told this young lady to come to her house at midnight on the night of a full moon."

The naïve girl followed the instructions that were passed on to her, and one night when the moon was full and the appointed time had arrived, the time of night popularly known to the old-time mountain folks as the "witching hour,"[4] she knocked on Amanda's door.

"She took the young lady to the attic," recalled the woman whose mother had known the participants first-hand.

---

3. Ibid.

4. Merriam-Webster.com Dictionary, Merriam-Webster, https://www.merriam-webster.com/dictionary/the%20witching%20hour.

"Fleeing From the Witch," near Beaver Dam, Centre County (drawn by James J. Frazier).

"There were two big black kettles there, and something was boiling in each one of them. And the witch Amanda said to the young lady, 'You must swear yourself to the devil and renounce God!'

That was more than the nervous girl could stand. Supernatural benefits be damned, she decided on the spot that they were not worth the sacrifices that she would have to make to gain the powers she had thought would be such fun. Probably without as much as a "good night" the frightened novitiate ran out of the house and into the ghostly light of the full moon, no doubt making it home in record time. It was an experience that she never cared to repeat, and her desire to pursue such aspirations was apparently satisfied because, noted our storyteller, "she never did become a witch."[5]

The story of the Beaver Dam witch contains several of the most common motifs that could once be found in the lore and legends of witchcraft throughout Pennsylvania. One of the most common of these motifs was the idea that a witch can't step over a broom, and even as late as 1988 I could talk to people who either believed in the idea themselves or who, in their lifetime, had known someone else who did.

---

5. Helen Elder (born 1921), recorded June 5, 1998.

"They always said, you know, if you suspected anybody of being a witch, a witch wouldn't step over a broom if you laid a broom down," recalled one lady who classified the belief as just an old superstition, and who didn't know any good stories about such incidents.[6] On the other hand, another gentleman I interviewed had a different idea about the belief, regarding it as more than just an old tall tale.

"I used to hear granddad talk about that," noted the ridge runner who remembered a lot about such matters.

"He said, 'Never step over a broom. It's bad luck to step over a broom.'" continued the entertaining storyteller.

"Well, I've stepped over a lot of 'em. I don't know what the difference is in steppin' over it, [but] I know they [witches] won't step over a broom. That's one thing they're definitely scared of. They won't step over a broom. I don't know why."[7]

Some decades earlier this same man suspected that two of his neighbors, a husband and wife in Centre County, were witches. The valley where he and his neighbors lived was sparsely populated about that time, and even just thirty years ago this same valley was still relatively unsettled, inhabited mostly by people who had been there all their lives. As a result, there were folks who were about sixty years behind the times when it came to modern ways of thinking, and they liked it that way, even though it meant accusing their neighbor of being a witch.

In this case, the accused, a woman and her husband, had descended from families who had reputations as practitioners of the black arts, and people thought the couple was still carrying on the tradition. All sorts of sensational stories were circulated about the acts of witchcraft perpetrated by these two people, and in order to prove to himself that the stories were true, the believer in the broom test decided to use it to unmask the witches.

"I tried that when they first said about it, and I didn't believe it!" explained the man who conducted the test.

"Them two people come here, and neither one of 'em would ever step over that broom! I'd lay it there on purpose to see if they'd step over it. They'd never step over the broom. They'd always reach down and pick it up!"[8]

6. Evelyn Breon (born 1918), recorded May 5, 1988.
7. Ray Rowles (born 1933), recorded May 26, 1988.
8. Ibid.

The old couple lived out their entire lives in the same valley, seemingly unconcerned about or unaware of the rumors that painted them as witches, and today no one there probably even remembers the tales about them anymore (I have not given the name of the valley because the woman is, to the best of my knowledge, still—in 1999—alive and living there yet).

"Time heals all wounds," or so claims the old adage, and in this case it was probably true. As the years passed, the accusations about the two reputed witches were gradually forgotten, and the man and his wife were able to live out their lives in peace. However, as some people living around Coburn and Spring Mills today will attest, it's not always that simple.

Spring Mills can boast of a famous braucher all its own. There are many stories that still survive about his powers, and about the great deal of good he was able to accomplish when he exercised those powers during the first half of the twentieth century.

Benny Ripka's name has come up before in previous tales included in the author's *Pennsylvania Fireside Tales* books, and his name will come up again in future volumes. He was considered to be quite the master at removing spells placed on people or on animals by hexes, or so many folks thought, and anecdotes about him are still recalled by local residents.

Those same tales also relate that while he was at the business of lifting spells, Benny also could divine the individual who cast the spell in the first place, or so he claimed. Benny's divinations, in at least one case however, caused a family feud that still divides members of that same family today. The family rift that Benny unintentionally spawned arose from his use of the broom test that was thought to be so effective in forcing a witch's hand. The time the incident occurred was during August of 1953.

"My stepmother had twin girls, and one twin died," recalled Benny's great granddaughter in 1999.

"Apparently Grandpa Ripka was there, and he laid a broom across the door, and he said, 'The next person to come in and pick up the broom, there's the one that bewitched and killed the baby!'

"Well, my one aunt went in and picked up the broom! It caused a big family feud, which still lasts to this day. A lot of family still don't talk because of that. Grudges carry very deep in the valley!"[9]

---

9. Nedra Meyer, recorded June 6, 1999.

I'm sure readers of this volume never imagined that belief in witches and witchcraft lingered in Pennsylvania as long as it did, but such deep-rooted impressions tend to survive, and among those were the supposed connections between witches and broomsticks.

Scholars say that the ancient Teutonic races held the belief that the broom was sacred to their god Odin, and that they also believed him to be the "ruler of the winds" and the composer of the "song of the storm." These same scholars, taking this a step further by blending these two ideas, go on to say that the superstition about witches riding broomsticks may be nothing more than an imaginative personification of "light scudding clouds that pass rapidly across the sky and herald squally weather."[10]

The scholars are probably correct in their analyses; the connections between witches, broomsticks, and weather do have their origins in mankind's earliest attempts to explain the weather and its vagaries. Moreover, the theory might indeed explain the reason why the Delawares once believed that high winds were portended by clouds they referred to as "witch's brooms."[11] Apparently the legends of the white people eventually intermixed with and colored even the Delawares' weather lore!

Despite the logical explanations for such beliefs, there are always diehards who cannot change the way they think, and even today we hear of devil worshipers who defile churches in their misguided attempts to follow the path of ancient superstition. At least, however, none of them are reported to have tried to ride a broomstick like a diehard in Centre County once attempted to do.

Mary Knoffsinger lived in Greens Valley, on top of Nittany Mountain near the village of Pleasant Gap, Centre County, "back in the 1800s." Apparently, she possessed some ancient tomes that contained the most potent formulae in a witch's armory, or so she must have thought.

Convinced that sources like the *Sixth and Seventh Books of Moses*, and other diabolical tools of hexerei, were as true as the passages contained in the Bible, this ardent believer one day decided to put the wizardry to a test.

"She made a salve out of three or four kinds of weeds or herbs, you know," recalled the life-long Greens Valley native who had heard the tale from his father. "And she got straddle a broom handle and smeared that

---

10. Charles Hardwick, *Traditions, Superstitions, and Folk-lore*, 117.
11. Gladys Tantaquidgeon, *Folk Medicine of the Delaware*, 90.

The Ebert Homestead as it looks today.

stuff around the broom handle. She got on the porch roof and said 'Good-bye'. She waved goodbye; she was gonna fly away!"[12]

The ninety-two-year-old gentleman paused a moment, with the witch straddling her broomstick, and we waited expectantly for him to continue. I had heard a similar tale from Professor Sam Bayard of Penn State University but had never gotten a chance to ask him follow-up questions about it.

He had been given the story down in Greene County when he was collecting folk tunes there during the 1930s, and it's worth repeating here, even though we have to leave the Greens Valley witch poised on the edge of her porch roof.

The woman who told Bayard the tale said she "was going to visit a friend," who lived in Monongalia County, West Virginia, just across the Pennsylvania line from the Pennsylvania towns of New Freeport and Brave.

"She was walking along the road and approaching the house," recounted Bayard, recalling the story that the woman had told to him in all serious-ness. "There was a fairly high wind, and she saw the person out in the front yard or barnyard close to a shed, and called to her; and instead of answering, the person simply took wing, as it were, or rather flew up over the shed, to the horror of this lady!"[13]

---

12. Dave Bilger (born 1907), recorded December 26, 1977.
13. Samuel P. Bayard (born 1908), recorded December 26, 1977.

Of course, a person's imagination can be very easily fooled into causing them to see things that aren't exactly what they think they are, and probably the most powerful effect the old beliefs in witchcraft had on people was the way they could cloud peoples' thoughts. These types of influences would explain how some of the more sensational parts of the story about the Beaver Dam witch arose.

However, in the case of the Greens Valley witch, even the strongest beliefs weren't powerful enough to overcome the force of gravity. The would-be flyer in Greens Valley did indeed become airborne, "but," concluded our storyteller, chuckling heartily to himself as he finished his tale, "she jumped off the porch roof and dang near killed herself."[14]

NOTE: With regards to the dam the beavers built at Beaver Dam before a town of that name grew up there, eighty-seven year old Clarence Musser, born in 1884, and who I interviewed in 1971, said that he had always heard that the beavers' dam was so large and so sturdy that people actually found that they could use it as a bridge, often driving their horses and wagons over it to cross the creek!

---

14. Bilger, Ibid.

CHAPTER IV

BEAR TRACKS

When a two-hundred-pound Centre County black bear wandered into downtown State College in search of food one December night in 1999 it caused quite a stir. First the errant bruin walked through a busy parking garage, and then, deciding to get a less-harried base of operations, climbed a tree in front of a florist shop on Allen Street.

After dealing with the crowds that gathered to watch the animal, and with the accompanying traffic congestion that followed, local police and state Game Commission officials were finally able to tranquilize the beast and transport it to a remote area. Here the sleepy bear was released so it could roam freely once more.

The officers from the Game Commission were later interviewed for a newspaper article about the event and were quoted as saying that anyone coming across a bear should not attempt to feed it; but should scare it away instead. This, they said, could "usually" be done by "clapping your hands and hollering."[1]

Not everyone confronted by a bear would feel comfortable resorting to noise as a method of chasing it off if the procedure doesn't always work, but the blame should not be placed upon the tactics. Rather the fault lies with the bears themselves, since, by nature, they are a rather unpredictable lot.

When a bear encounters a man out in the wild its reaction can range from frighteningly surly to positively comical. It might be said such behavior is motivated by the lack of respect that the human race has shown the

---

1. Erin R. Wengerd, "Black Bear Checks Out Downtown, Climbs a Tree," *Centre Daily Times*, State College, PA, December 6, 1999.

ursine family over the centuries; which has caused old bruin to be as fickle as he acts sometimes when he meets one of us. Not an explanation that's likely to be true, since it's an animal's inherent traits that dictate its behavior, but one that does seem to be supported when hunters talk about their face-to-face encounters with these large carnivores.

Meshach Browning, that great nimrod of the southern Alleghenies of Southwestern Pennsylvania, Maryland, and West Virginia from 1795 to 1839, claimed that during one hunting season he "saw twenty bears." Of these, he, by his own account, "killed seventeen, and wounded one," with the last one getting away since it was "shot a little before dark."[2]

Other hunters were just as merciless. Up in the mountains around present-day Scranton, Elias Scott was making his mark as the nimrod of the Lackawanna Valley about the same time that Meshach Browning roamed the mountains to the south. Accustomed to taking long hunting trips in the fall, Scott would be gone for up to a week at a time when he went on one of his solitary hunts.

When evening came the hardy mountain man would build a campfire to keep wolves and other wild animals at bay. Once his fire was blazing, Scott would settle down for the night, his hunting knife and musket by his side, and his leather knapsack rolled up for a pillow.

On one of his expeditions Scott spent the night encamped along the banks of Stafford Meadow Brook in the Moosic Mountains south of Scranton. At daybreak the avid hunter arose and started off into the woods, but he wasn't the only early riser that morning. He hadn't gone too far before he spotted a bear contentedly eating some berries for breakfast. Thinking it would be an easy kill, the marksman aimed and fired.

The bullet found its mark, but it was not a fatal shot, and the enraged bear closed on his assailant. Unable to load his musket before the bear attacked, Scott used the rifle to fend off the enraged animal, backing away from it the whole time.

This proved to be an effective defense until the hunter's boot caught on a root, causing him to trip and to fall down. The bear was upon him in an instant, grabbing his left hand in its mouth. Then there took place, in that lonely spot in the mountains, a death struggle between man and beast.

---

2. Meshach Browning, *Forty-Four Years of the Life of a Hunter*, 152.

With a presence of mind that came from his many years of taking care of himself in the forest, Scott was able to grab his trusty knife with his free hand and used it to stab the huge bear that was on top of him. This he continued to do until the animal had lost so much blood that "he fell dead upon the mangled hunter."[3]

Aaron Hall was another determined bear hunter who proved to be more than a match for any bear that crossed his path. Born in 1828 in a log cabin that sat along Dick's Run in Centre County, Hall eventually settled along a remote section of the Rattlesnake Pike on the Allegheny Mountains above Unionville. His hunting tactics were much like that of Elias Scott's, and Hall's descendants relate that the old hunter died of pneumonia contracted from nights of sleeping out in cold weather on one of his protracted expeditions.

That same Hall family oral tradition recounts the story of one such outing which involved a bear that left tracks that the avid hunter could easily follow. Once he was on a track, Hall was apparently not one to give up until he had killed the animal he was pursuing. In this notable case it's recalled that he trailed the bear all the way to the Bear Meadows, today a state natural area preserved near the town of Tusseyville. It was a trek of at least twelve miles, and probably a good bit further since the twelve miles would be the distance measured, as they say in the mountains, as the crow flies.

Hall shot the bear somewhere in the Bear Meadows forestland and then had to decide what to do with it. Family accounts say the energetic mountaineer "went and got it in the wagon," but it's not clear whose wagon. If it was his own, Hall would have had to hike all the way back to Unionville, hitch up his horse and wagon, and then return to the Bear Meadows to get his bear. It would not have been an impossible feat for a man who was used to long hikes in the rugged hills around his brick mansion, which still stands today along the Rattlesnake Pike.[4]

Old-time hunter Laroy Lyman, born in 1821, was yet another nimrod who never gave the bears a rest. By his own account, Lyman estimated he "killed about 3,000 deer and over 400 bear" during his many years of

3. Hollister, *History of the Lackawanna Valley*, 282.
4. Ellis Hall (born 1919), recorded August 7, 1999.

hunting.[5] Lyman, a nationally known hunter whose homestead was located in Roulette, Potter County, kept a diary of his many hunting exploits, and in that interesting journal he mentions his encounters with the bears of the Black Forest of northern Pennsylvania.

However, none of these records stand out as a particularly notable bear story worth mentioning in this chapter. The diary's entries are succinct and matter-of-fact, each one just another day in the ordinary life of this rugged mountaineer and old-time hunter. On the other hand, there were apparently some episodes that Lyman chose, for one reason or another, not to include in his personal accounts.

For those stories it is necessary to turn to the oral history handed down through the descendants of the great hunter. When those sources are consulted there seems to be one unusual bear that Lyman was apparently fond of talking about repeatedly. It is a story that was remembered by his children and passed on to his grandchildren, who in turn wrote it down for theirs.

According to that archived account, the "peculiar ways and comic habits" of black bears in general were a continuing source of amusement and wonder for the avid nimrod. Nonetheless there was one bear in particular, one that seemed far wiser and more comical than the others, that intrigued him the most. It was often this one that he talked about when telling his bear stories.

A surprising choice since, despite his many attempts to shoot and trap this particular bear, Lyman always seemed to be outwitted by the wily bruin. Then one day the frustrated hunter devised a plan for a set-up that he felt sure would net him the quarry that had eluded him for so long.

First, he built a three-sided enclosure consisting of "crude rail fences," and concealed his bear trap in the middle of the enclosure. He decided not to use bait in the trap, thinking that this would only warn the cagey old beast that something was amiss. Instead, Lyman decided to rely on the natural curiosity of the creature to lure him in.

In addition, to increase the appeal of the setup, Laroy also placed one of his old high hats on a stake he had driven into the ground right behind

___

5. Robert R. Lyman Sr., *History of Roulet, Pennsylvania*, 83. Details on Laroy Lyman's life and times were also obtained from a copy of his personal diary and memoirs. Laroy's personal estimate of his hunting record, p.4, copy loaned to author by Lyman's great-granddaughter, Ms. Krista Lyman of Roulette.

the concealed trap. This interesting fixture, he hoped, would tweak the bear's curiosity even more, leading it right into the trap.

The next morning the would-be trapper returned to his elaborate snare, hoping to see that the old bear's curiosity had led to its entrapment. As he approached the site of the enclosure he strained to see if the bear had been caught, and then, on the road ahead, he saw a pile of wooden rails. Perched on top was the bear, with the high hat sitting at a cocked angle on its head.

Lyman "instantly" knew that the old bruin had detected the trap, disassembled it, and dragged the rails out onto the road. He also had placed Lyman's top hat on its head as a final outrageous way to mock his adversary. Then, with Lyman looking on, the bear took off the hat, placed it on the top rail and sat on it. The head gear was smashed flat as a pancake, almost as though the bear did it to add insult to injury.

The written account concludes by noting that the trapper was so astonished at the sight in front of him that he didn't have time to shoot at the bear when it scrambled down off the wood pile and walked off into the forest.[6] Although it could be argued that this episode might have been a story that Laroy Lyman made up to entertain his grandchildren or to tell fellow old-timers when they gathered to spin their yarns around the pot-belly stove at Lyman's General Store in Roulet, there are others whose encounters with bears sound just as fantastic.

One such tale is the story of Henry Eyer of Pine Mountain, Clinton County. Born in 1876, "Hen" Eyer eventually took up agriculture as his livelihood, turning his one-hundred-ten-acre farm at the head of Spring Run into a garden spot. In his younger days, however, the young Clinton Countian farmed Pine Mountain lands owned by a man named Sam Motter.

"California Sam," so named because of money he inherited from his father out in California, was a local character. Motter loved roaming the forests, seemingly preferring the solitude they offered rather than the company of his fellow man. However, he also enjoyed doing outrageous things just to see peoples' reactions, like the time he decided to bridle a bear he had caught in a trap.

Around 1907 or 1908, Motter placed some bear traps out along Robbins Road, near the cranberry swamp, east of the Pine-Loganton Road on

---

6. Ibid, Lyman diary, 6.

top of Pine Mountain. The traps were the typical steel jaw variety, and they proved to be effective, netting at least two bears for the trapper.

Motter wanted to take home a live specimen, but the first one bit down on his leg as he was trying to release it. In order to free himself, he hit the bear on the head with a hatchet he was carrying, but he misjudged the strength of his blow, striking the bruin so hard that it died on the spot. He didn't have much better luck with the second one.

The second bear had its foot securely caught in the jaws of another of his traps when Motter discovered it. Rather than using the same approach that he had tried on the first bear, Sam Motter went home and asked his young farmhand to come along back. With them the two men carried a bridle and some ropes, the plan being that Sam would attract the bear's attention on one side while young Eyer was to sneak up on the other. Then, according to Motter's instructions, he was to "grab that bear by the ears and get that bridle on before he bites you."

"So dad said Sam attracted the bear," recalled Hen Eyer's son, who heard the tale from his father. "He said this bear was looking towards Sam, and he said I snuck up alongside him there, and I grabbed him by the ears; and he said I got the bridle in his mouth."

The two men managed to tighten the bridle, get a rope on the bear, and prod and pull it out to the nearest public road on the mountain. Here they tied it to a tree, and Motter brought it some food and water.

It was only a few days before bear season, and Motter wanted to walk his bridled specimen through the streets of Loganton just to show off. However, within a day or two the bear was dead, frightened to death, thought Hen Eyer, from the trauma of its capture. It was a tale the old mountaineer would often tell his son in later years, and that same son assured me that he didn't think his dad "would tell a lie."[7]

In most cases it is the bear that frightens the man, rather than the opposite, but the bear is usually alive when this happens. However, about fifty years ago over in the mountains above Nippenose Valley, Lycoming County, there was a solitary hunter who was almost frightened to death by the bear he had just shot and gutted.

It was not a very big bear, between a hundred and a hundred fifty pounds, and the hunter, who "was pretty wiry at that stage of his life,"

---

7. Alvin Eyer (born 1915), recorded August 14, 1999.

decided to carry it off the mountain, rather than drag it and risk ruining the hide.

"So, what he did, he tied all four feet together with the dragging rope, and then he got down and he put his head up between the feet and he put it on like a knapsack," recalled the hunter's friend. "So then, he emptied his rifle, and he was carrying his rifle and he had this bear and its legs around his neck. And the bear itself is around behind him. He'd gutted it, but he didn't take the lungs or anything out—the lungs or liver; he just took the entrails out."

The determined hunter started back down the mountain with his burden on his back, making good time until he came to a "big blowdown log" that had fallen across the path. "It was quite a chore to step up on with this added weight, but he finally got himself balanced and up on this log," continued our storyteller.

"Well, then the easiest way down was, he thought, just jump down. You know, just sort of land on both feet. Well, when he did, the bear swung and come back again' him and forced the air out of the lungs. Its head was layin' right there by his ear, and it went 'Woof' into his ear!

"And he said, 'Did you ever see a grown man throw a rifle and run? I just threw the rifle and took off! No matter how fast I run, I wasn't puttin' any distance between the bear and me. It was right with me the whole time!'"[8]

Our storyteller didn't mention at what point the hunter realized he was running from a dead bear still strapped to his back, but it was probably after the man ran out of breath and could go no further. Later the bear killer could laugh about the incident, perhaps thinking that bears could indeed be unpredictable, even when they were dead.

Bears have never lost their ability to frighten and amuse people with their unpredictable antics. One October evening about twenty-two years ago a young squirrel hunter was returning to a hunting camp located up in Voneida Gap north of Big Poe Mountain, Centre County, when he noticed a huge black bear sitting in a laurel thicket up ahead.

At first it didn't alarm the man, since the bear didn't appear to be interested in him. It was almost cute, "sittin' there like a teddy bear; just lookin' around like a big teddy bear would sit on your bed," recalled the man who saw it. He could also see his cabin only a hundred yards ahead, with the

---

8. Dave Poust (born 1930), recorded June 21, 1998.

reassuring glow from a lantern on a table inside shining through the windows. Then the bear came down out of the laurel thicket and got between the man and the hunting camp.

It was a sight he still remembers to this day. "When I looked at his legs they looked like eight-inch stove pipes," he recalls; "I estimated him to be four-hundred to four-hundred-and-fifty pounds! It was all black except for one big patch of white on its chest."

The bear was the same one the other hunters at the camp had been seeing off and on that year, and now it sat on the road in front of him just sizing him up. Finally, the monster got up and lumbered in his direction. It was then that the hunter fully appreciated the bear's size, noticing that it was so massive that "when he walked he just shook!"

Hoping that the bear would not come closer, the frightened nimrod just froze, until the bear came within five yards and stopped. While shifting its weight from side-to-side, the animal eyed the human, snorting at him several times.

"When he did that, that raised the hair on back of my neck," laughed the hunter who experienced the hair-raising episode, and who also recalled that the bear would not let him pass, no matter if he walked left or right when trying to circle around it. At one point the animal rose up on its hind legs and came within three yards of the man, who then pointed his twenty-two-magnum rifle at the beast after trying unsuccessfully to scare it away by hollering at it.

However, realizing that a rifle this small was "not much killing power for a bear," the cornered hunter lowered his weapon and kept edging around the bruin. Finally, he managed to get ahead of his antagonist and into a hemlock clearing, at which point his plan of escape became clearer as well.

"I decided "if he's gonna get me now, he's gonna get me from behind!" claimed the lucky escapee. From there it was a mad dash onto the porch and through the cabin door to safety.

The bear didn't linger around the camp once its prey was inside, and no one ever saw it around there again; nor did anyone ever hear of its being shot. By now it's no doubt dead from old age, but its descendants are probably the bears that inhabit the same forest today and which people still see from time to time as they drive through the wilds of Voneida Gap.[9]

---

9. Lance Arney (born 1950), recorded July 4, 2000.

Bears can be as curious as cats, as the fortunate Voneida Gap hunter now knows, and their curiosity often draws them to humans who would just as soon see them mind their own business. One Clinton County buck hunter certainly still feels that way after inadvertently drawing a curious bear to him one October day during archery season about ten years ago. He had splashed some buck lure, "Tink's Number 69," on his boots, and it was early in the morning.

"It was just getting light enough to see maybe ten feet," began the archer. "I was just starting to put tree steps into a tree when I heard this noise coming. I figured 'here's one coming in already', thinking a buck was coming. Then I could see it was a black bear!"

It wasn't a big bear, somewhere around one-hundred-fifty to one-hundred-seventy pounds, but it was fearless. Hollering, and throwing sticks and stones at it didn't seem to bother the bruin in the least, and it got to within ten yards of the hunter before he beat a hasty retreat, leaving his bow, arrows, and a fanny pack with the bottle of Tink's 69 in it, lying beside the tree.

After "waiting him out," the hunter assumed the bear had followed him because of the buck lure it smelled on his boots. His assumption proved to be correct since, when he was finally able to retrieve his pack and bow, he found that the animal had chewed through the pack and then on the seductive bottle of lure, leaving marks from its big teeth on both. Although dismayed at the time that he had lost a morning's hunt because of the bear, it was an experience the archer will never forget and an episode which he now classifies as "a pretty interesting morning" after all.[10]

Another interesting time was had by a hiker who was walking on a mountain in Centre County during the summer of 2000. He had ventured into one of the wildest parts of southern Centre County, where Tussey Mountain and Thick Head Mountain come together to form an inviting array of airy glens and dark hollows choked with mountain laurel and hemlocks. Once there he continued into a spot that even now seems more romantic and more untamed than all the others.

The name of this deep hollow is Treaster Kettle, a title that conjures up images of the Hatfield and McCoy country of West Virginia and Kentucky. Although never the scene of feuds like the Hatfield-McCoy wars, it is to

10. Richard Sodergren (born 1942), recorded May 12, 2000.

this day a place where peace and seclusion can be had by anyone who chooses to penetrate into this mini-wilderness. Even the bears here seem placid at times; at least that seemed to be the case with the black bear that walked through here that one summer in 2000.

The solitary hiker spotted the bruin directly ahead on the Treaster Kettle Road. It was about two hundred yards away when he first saw it, and he figured it would run away when it saw him. However, the bear kept walking towards him, until it got to within thirty steps, at which point the hiker hollered and threw a handful of crushed stone at it, both to no avail. To the hiker's surprise, the beast kept on coming and then passed by him, not even turning its head to acknowledge his presence, as though the human was of a lower social class unworthy of even a passing glance.

It appeared the bear had been injured. Its right hip and the right side of its head were "all scarred up," perhaps from a fight with another bear or from being hit by a car. After passing the man, the animal almost immediately left the road and disappeared into the forest, but the experience was still a frightening one. Looking back, the hiker now recalls that the beast "looked like it weighed two hundred pounds after it passed, but six hundred when it was coming towards me!"[11]

The Treaster Kettle hiker wasn't drinking when he saw the bear on the road ahead, but if he had been, the large beast may have looked even bigger when it was approaching. Hard to say what the bear may have thought the human looked like if it had been drinking, but about fifty years ago a group of men would sometimes bring a pet bear to the bar at Orner's Hotel in Milroy, Mifflin County, and let it drink beer.

The Potlicker Flats men who owned the bear, and the other bar patrons, would "get it boomed up," and then, as the evening's form of entertainment, watch the bear stagger around. It was an ironic turn of events given the fact that the bear's tormentors came from Potlicker Flats, so-named because of the one-time prevalence of moonshine stills in that section.

Given that fact, it could even be said that old bruin, if he had been more intelligent, might have thought that his race indeed gets no respect from the human one. On the other hand, according to the man who recalled seeing the inebriated men load the drunken bear onto the back

---

11. Gil Ralston (born 1923), recorded September 12, 2000.

of their truck when it was time to go home, they "weren't in much better shape than the bear!"[12]

It turns out that the Mifflin County men were not unique in their fun-loving antics. Earlier Pennsylvania hunters and outdoorsmen also found bears to be a source of adrenaline-pumping amusement as well. One such group of thrill seekers lived in the Pine Creek Valley of Lycoming County in the first decade of the nineteenth century.

Here, in 1805, a large group of young men and women had gone out to pick whortleberries (also once referred to as the "Pennsylvania blueberry"), and in the course of their activities they spotted a young bear greedily eating the berries in the same patch.

Several virile young stalwarts in the group decided that the bear might afford them a good opportunity to impress their lady friends, particularly since they had all brought along their dogs. They dogs were all good hunting dogs, and so men and dogs immediately gave chase.

They soon had the bear up a tree, but it had climbed too high for what the men had planned to do, and so they waited until it came back down. They continued the chase, forcing it up several other trees until they had it perched on one tree's lower limb, about fifteen feet off the ground.

One fellow said they should try to take the beast alive, but his suggestion was met with jeers and claims that it could not be done. Nonetheless, after some discussion it was agreed that they should at least give it a try, whereupon they began to fashion ropes from the inner bark they stripped off some cedar trees they found growing nearby.

Once they had sufficient cordage, the young swains made loops in the ends of the several lengths they had created. Next, they built and fastened a flimsy scaffolding onto the tree trunk, which was just high enough that one of the more daring chaps could climb it and look the bear in the eye.

He had also carried the ropes up with him, and once at the bear's height he managed to slip one noose around the bear's neck and another around one of its paws. The lassoed bear was then somehow driven back down to ground level, where it was kept under control with the ropes around it until the men managed to tie a long pole across its neck.

"In this manner we drove him a couple of miles," recalled one of the boys when an old man and writing his memoirs, "and after we concluded

---

12. Craig Weidensaul (born 1932), telephone interview August 8, 2000.

that he had given us sufficient amusement, we cut the ropes and set him at liberty." The old gentleman further noted that "Bears from six months to three years old can easily be taken in this manner, but the older ones are not so easily managed."[13]

The same old gentlemen also noted that January and February were the best times to hunt bears since those cold snowy months were the easiest time to track the bruins to their dens. Nonetheless, even then a hunter had to be adequately prepared to claim his trophy, with the best chance of success only afforded to those who were well-equipped with dogs and guns.

Once the bear had been tracked to its den in the rocks, a smart hunter would not even think of crawling in after it or having his dogs do so. Instead, he would also have brought sulfur cakes along with him, which he would ignite and throw into the dark recesses where the bear was hiding. After some time, the pungent and disagreeable smell of the burning sulfur, noted the old nimrod, "soon started them out."[14]

Today the black bear still finds the forests of Pennsylvania an agreeable place to live, with an estimated population of 20,000, but they are still sought out by many hunters who want to add them to their other trophies, as over 3,100 devotees of the chase were able to do in 2017.

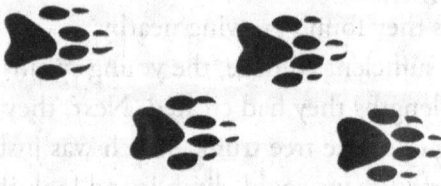

Bear tracks.

---

13. Philip Tome, *Pioneer Life or Thirty Years a Hunter*, 72.
14. Ibid.

CHAPTER V

THE LAST PACKS

During the terrible European wars of the 1600s, it's recorded that parts of Germany were so desolated by invading armies that "where once were flourishing farms and vineyards, now whole bands of wolves roamed unmolested."[1] Other European countries had bountiful wolf populations as well, with Ireland being particularly noted for prevalence of the wolves in the Emerald Isle; a distinction which gave it the less-welcome title of "Wolf-land."[2]

The only reason, some have conjectured, that wolves were so numerous all over Europe, even as late as the 1600s, was because monarchs and noblemen had wanted it that way for centuries. It was not the will of the people to have any wolves around at all, but the nobility had always enjoyed the sport and the recreation that hunting of the wily beasts provided, and so they passed strict laws protecting them.

Eventually these hated forest laws were changed or rescinded and wolf hunting became a common practice. So intense was the interest, so deep-seated the hatred of wolves, that special dogs were bred and trained to use in catching and killing them. The most well-known and effective of these "wolf dogs" came from Ireland, where, through interbreeding, the Irishmen developed a powerful canine of immense size and instincts that was particularly effective in scenting and attacking the species known to science as *Canis lupus*.

Gradually through the use of the Irish "wolf hound" and through other brutal measures, citizens of Europe began to decimate wolf populations,

1. Oscar Kuhns, *The German and Swiss Settlements of Colonial Pennsylvania*, 9.
2. James E. Harting, *Extinct British Animals*, 198–99.

and it wasn't more than a century or two before European wolves were almost extinct. And with their disappearance the stories of the slayers of the last wolves became celebrated topics of conversation, particularly since, as Stuart in his *Lays of the Deer Forest* (published in 1848) noted "Every district has its last wolf."[3]

Descendants of Rory Carragh, in County Tyrone, Ireland, are, no doubt, still proud of the fact that he is remembered as the hunter who killed the last wolf in that part of the Emerald Isle. Likewise in Scotland, one MacQueen of Pall-a-chrocain is heralded as the slayer of the last wolf in that country, and here in Pennsylvania there were individuals who can be awarded that distinction as well (see the chapter titled "Tough As Nails" in the author's *Pennsylvania Fireside Tales Volume VI* for interesting accounts of their wolf hunting exploits).

It is also interesting to look into the techniques used to whittle Pennsylvania wolf populations down to the point of extinction here in the Keystone State. It might be said that the saga of Pennsylvania's wolf hunting began with the first Swedish colonies along the Delaware River in 1643.

Plagued by wolves at every turn, historical records indicate that the resourceful Swedes "constructed 52 wolf pits to protect their livestock"[4], and in Charles II's 1681 Charter to William Penn it is stated that "each Towne bee obliged for the preservation of Stock and Cattle to make and maintain Wolve pitts which are to be directed by the respective Officers of the towns to which they belong."[5]

Wolf pits, or trapping pits, as they were first called in Europe, dated back to the Stone Age. They were normally just holes in the ground but sometimes were built from stone as well. In either case the pits could measure up to 13 by 23 feet and were often as deep as seven to twelve feet. The openings of the pits were cleverly concealed by branches and leaves, and the sides of the pits were steeply inclined outward.

The sides were also lined with wooden planks or masonry, and sometimes the bottoms of the pits contained sharpened sticks pointing upward. These traps were an extremely effective way of reducing the numbers of wolves in an area and one favored by bounty hunters. The construction of the pits made it impossible for wolves to escape once they fell in, and if the

---

3. Ibid, 177–78.

4. Wes Bower, "Three Centuries and Counting," *Pennsylvania Game News October 2010*, 6.

5. Charter to William Penn and Laws of the Province of Pennsylvania, 1681.

sharpened stakes at the bottom did not kill the wolves, they could easily be shot.

Although traces of those pits can no longer be found today, there is at least one landmark name in Michaux State Forest that perhaps preserves their memory; at least that's one conclusion that can be reached from the name Wolf Pit Hill that still appears on topographical maps of the South Mountains country. Although the wolf pits were a contributing factor in the decline of the wolf in Pennsylvania, in the end it was bounties that proved to be the driving force behind their extinction.

Monetary rewards for wolf pelts were introduced in Pennsylvania during the time of William Penn. He and his fellow Quakers established bounties in 1683, paying 50 to 75 cents per pelt, thereby creating a class of trappers and fur traders who made a living by pursuing this lucrative hunting trade. The bounties increased regularly until in 1802 they had risen to $8 for an adult and $2.50 for a pup, and by 1840 they went as high as $25 for an adult and $15 for a pup.[6]

Each Pennsylvania County seems to have its tale of at least one wolf bounty hunter or of someone who collected the bounty just because they happened to kill a wolf. In northern Pennsylvania, for example, there is an amusing account of a Seneca who killed a wolf in Cattaraugus County New York, just across the Pennsylvania line, sometime in the early 1800s. The Indian took the wolf's scalp to Meadville, Pennsylvania, to collect a bounty for it, but when he honestly confessed as to where he had shot it, the local magistrate told him it would not be lawful to pay him the bounty since the wolf had not been shot in Pennsylvania.

He "could not" he firmly stated, "pay for scalps taken out of the county." Somewhat perplexed and irritated, the quick-witted hunter replied that "It is bad law, because you require that the wolf should know the county lines. Had this wolf seen a flock of sheep just within the Pennsylvania lines I dare say he would not have stopped for the county lines!" Whereupon the magistrate "paid him the bounty of five dollars."[7]

Similarly, there is an account from Shade Township in Somerset County that tells of how William Oldham moved into that area in 1825 after purchasing 250 acres at 50 cents an acre. Oldham, who was known as an expert

---

6. Wes Bower, "Three Centuries and Counting," *Pennsylvania Game News October 2010*, 6.
7. *Native American Magazine*, NY.

hunter, was said to have paid for his land by hunting wolves and collecting the bounties paid for their pelts. It was told that he killed seven in one day; shooting six and then crawling into the wolf's den to kill the seventh.[8]

The last bounty paid for a wolf killed in Bucks County may have been paid to John Smith in 1800. The young trapper had been trapping foxes in Plumstead Township of that county, and one morning found one of his traps had disappeared. Judging from the tracks he could see that some sort of animal had been caught in it and had dragged it off.

Reluctant to lose his trap, Smith followed the tracks and soon discovered the trap's chain had been caught in a nearby stake and rider fence. Upon closer inspection he could see a large gray wolf caught in the trap itself. He ran home and excitedly told his father of his catch, whereupon the man grabbed his rifle and went off and shot the wolf. It's not recorded whether or not young Smith collected a bounty for his "catch of the day," but that very same trap was kept in the family. Handed down to succeeding generations, it may still be in their possession, where it's now no doubt cherished as a family heirloom.[9]

Prior to the time when only lone wolves remained in the state there were the last packs; the struggling families of the once-prevalent groups of predators that were so despised by the state's early settlers. Despite the settlers' determination to kill them all, even these last packs managed to survive well into the nineteenth century.

One such pack roamed the wilds of Snyder County for many years up until the winter of 1834. In the spring of the following year, when the heavy snows melted off Shade Mountain, this notorious pack was found frozen to death in a huddled mass. They had apparently died of starvation and from exposure to the unusually cold winter.

Other packs did not fare much better in subsequent years as poisoning, trapping, and hunting began to take their toll. Bounty hunting in particular encouraged many hunters to take up the chase and to devise new ways to increase their chances of killing a wolf, with ring hunting being one of the more unusual methods.

Ring hunts, sometimes called "great hunts," were used with varying degrees of success in killing large numbers of wolves and other predatory

---

8. William H. Welfley, *History of Bedford and Somerset Counties, Pennsylvania*, 410–11.
9. W. W. H. Davis, *The History of Bucks County, Pennsylvania*, 407.

animals within extensive areas. Some of these hunts could be quite success-ful at times, like the one that took place in Wyoming County one balmy June day in 1825.

Settlers there were tired of losing their domestic animals to wolves and other predators, and they finally decided to do something about it. A day was chosen for the great hunt, and when the day came about six hundred farmers, hunters, and other country folk gathered in the chosen spot.

With them they carried their guns, axes, hatchets, knives, pitchforks, and anything else that they thought might be useful in killing an animal. Each man also carried enough food to last several days, and at a given signal they all branched out so that in the end they encircled an area of over one hundred square miles of unbroken wilderness.

Then, at the sound of another agreed-upon signal, the men began to converge toward the center of their circle, beating the brush and making as much noise as they could in other ways. By the end of the second day, they had scared most the wildlife out of its hiding places and the circle was small enough that "every man had plenty of action." The non-predatory creatures like rabbits and deer were ignored as the slaughter of the bigger animals continued unabated for hours.

When it was finally over the great hunt was hailed as a success with a count of seventy-two panthers, ninety wolves, one hundred forty-five bears, thirty-seven foxes, and twenty-eight wildcats put down as the final tally. All the animals were skinned and the hides sold to fur buyers for a total of twenty-five-hundred dollars, while bounties on the wolves and panthers netted another three hundred fifty dollars from the state. Each hunter took home about $5.00 for their two days' work and also received thirty-five pounds of bear meat after it was divided up evenly.[10]

A similar hunt was conducted in Bradford County in 1818 when seven hundred hunters gathered in Wysox Township one day. After the men formed a ring of about 150 square miles, a horn was blown from atop Frenchtown Mountain. It in turn was answered by all the other horns in the circle, a reveille, it's recalled, which "lasted a full fifteen minutes."[11]

10. Breth Harris, WKDKA Pittsburgh radio show "Historical Program," February 10, 1944, transcript given to author by Harris Breth; Also see David Craft, *History of Bradford County, Pennsylvania*, 255–56.

11. Breth Harris, WKDKA Pittsburgh radio show "A Hunting We Will Go," January 15, 1944, transcript given to author by Harris Breth.

As the men began to close the circle, they slowly squeezed together a large number of all kinds of wild animals. Soon riflemen were taking aim at darting deer, streaking foxes, and racing panthers, and the crackle of musket fire went on without interruption for hours.

Eventually the circle became too small for the men to fire their weapons safely, at which point they began to use the other weapons they had brought with them, including bayonets fixed on poles, clubs, pitchforks, and similar items. Finally, when there was no game left to kill, the hunters counted three-hundred deer, five bears, nine wolves, and eleven foxes lying dead.

Not a tally as high as that in Wyoming County, but all present considered the event a great success despite the fact that it was estimated that "five-hundred deer, ten bears, and twenty wolves had escaped, along with a great number of smaller animals."[12]

Hunters in Clinton County could not paint such a rosy picture of their success when they conducted a ring hunt there in the fall of 1849. It was said that up until that time no other event had caused so much excitement in Beech Creek Township, with over three hundred hunters from all over the county jamming the streets of Beech Creek that day.

All would-be participants of the great hunt were enthused about getting a chance to rid the surrounding countryside of the overabundance of the predators that were a continual nuisance to local farmers. Word had spread as to how the hunt was to be executed and the weapons needed by those who would like to take part, and so the men had brought their guns as well as weapons for "hand-to-hand" combat.

As a result, those who came just to satisfy their curiosity could see hunters wielding pitchforks, hickory poles with bayonets attached, pike-poles, and even some fishing spears. It was an army that was not prepared to give quarter to anything, but the organizers of the hunt decided only six men, the most expert marksmen, should carry guns.

The men were divided into two columns, with all but the six chosen marksmen leaving their guns behind, much to the disgust of most of them. They put aside their irritation, however, and picked up their other weapons and headed for the Tangascootac Valley, where they were to gather at a clearing known as the David Improvement five miles northwest of Beech Creek.

---

12. Harris, Ibid.

The two columns were to march within half a mile of the clearing, and, once there, spit up and form a circle around it. The plan went off without a hitch with the formed circle being about two miles wide. Once the circle had been formed, a hunting horn was blown to signal that the hunters could begin closing the loop. Enthusiasm began to swell as the men began to anticipate the big game that they were entrapping, including panthers, wolves, deer, and bear. The six marksmen primed their muskets and held them ready since they were to kill as many of the animals as they could before the others pitched in.

Making as much noise as they could and waving their weapons in the most intimidating fashion they could muster, the men closed in toward the center. As they got closer and closer they became more and more excited since they could see many different animals trapped in the ring. However, they were to soon learn that they had not yet mastered the art of ring hunting.

There was a system which all participants in a ring hunt had to follow to prevent gaps in the ring, but it was not in place that day. Wide gaps appeared in the circle and at one breach as many as seven deer made it out. By the time all the holes had been closed there wasn't, much to the chagrin of the hunters, a single wild animal left inside. The entire party sheepishly came back down the mountain empty-handed "fully convinced that they did not understand ring hunting."[13]

Ever afterwards, as though to add insult to injury, the great hunting ground where the ring hunt fiasco occurred was derisively referred to as "the great slaughtering ground," and to this day topographical maps of the area show a trail through here called the "Slaughtering Ground Trail." Those hunters who took part in the hunt must have laid low afterwards since they probably felt that they would "never live that one down."

Sometime the circle hunts would be organized solely for the purpose of ridding an area of wolves, just like the ring hunt another group of Clinton County hunters conducted in the autumn of 1819 around the village of Lamar. This one too was not an event they would later want to recall but one which they felt they had to conduct since the wolves in the area were taking such a heavy toll on their livestock.

---

13. John Blair Linn, *History of Centre and Clinton Counties Pennsylvania*, 578.

The hunt was organized and conducted much like the Beech Creek hunt of 1849, with enthusiastic participants wielding muskets, pitchforks, and the like. Starting with a circle several miles wide, the hunters began closing in at the sound of a hunting horn. Amid much noise and blustering they finally could see the terror-filled game they had managed to trap—one confused and frightened rabbit.[14]

Despite some notable failures, a large amount of successful wolf hunting occurred in Pennsylvania, and it was certainly an important cause of the wolf's extermination. On the other hand, sporadic hunting was not the primary reason that the wolf finally disappeared from the Keystone State. It was once the state government started to offer attractive bounties for wolf hides that bounty hunting marked the beginning of the end for the wolf in Pennsylvania.

A twenty-five-dollar bounty was enough incentive for a wolf hunter to kill all the wolves he could find, but there are rotten apples in every barrel and some so-called wolf hunters tried to scam the system in whatever ways they could. As one early Pennsylvania biologist put it in 1896, "It is true that the bounty records in different counties of the state, as late as perhaps six months ago, show that wolf scalps have been paid for. Such data, however, must not be taken as conclusive evidence of the presence of these animals, for the heads and ears of grizzly, long-haired cur dogs, etc., or the pelts of wolves brought to Pennsylvania from other states, have in past years proven of considerable value to scalp hunters, although expensive to the local taxpayers."[15]

It seems to be now widely acknowledged, however, that dogs here in Pennsylvania had something to do with the extermination of the state's wolves after all. Apparently, around 1850 dogs with hydrophobia passed the disease on to their canine cousins, which gradually weakened the wolves' breeding stock. This epidemic, coupled with the other merciless methods of wolf extermination, and by man's unregulated slaughter of wild game and destruction of habitat from heavy lumbering operations, finally caused the collapse of the wolf population. Gradually all that remained were a few stragglers that were finally killed off as the "last wolves," and their stories appear in the next chapter.

---

14. Ibid, 630.
15. Samuel N. Rhoads, *Mammals of Pennsylvania and New Jersey,* 149.

Wolves in their neatly kept pens. They can be seen today at The Wolf Sanctuary near Lititz in Lancaster County. The caretakers here are dedicated to saving abandoned wolf pets and injured wolves found in the wild (photos taken in October of 2018 by the author).

CHAPTER VI

WOLF MARAUDERS

Although I had all but given up on finding anymore old-time wolf stories in my interviewing and research, I have, much to my delight, recently discovered several wolf tales I had collected in the past, but which had somehow gotten misfiled in my study. It is these episodes I want to share with my readers in this new *Volume VIII* chapter, since the time in Pennsylvania's past when wolves were an everyday threat is a thrilling one that deserves a compiler.

As one early Cambria County historian put it in writing of the times of the first settlers in that county, "There were at that time no roads through the wilderness to older settlements, and nothing but canoes for navigating the streams. Beasts of burden were rare, but wild beasts of the forest were quite numerous. Panthers, wolves, bears, etc., howled at night around the cabins of settlers."[1]

It was also true that, as one of those early borderers once put it, "Nothing among the wild beasts strikes such terror to the heart of the settler as the cry of the wolf at a lonely spot at night."[2]

The settlers over in western Pennsylvania would have been among the first to agree with that assessment, including the family of early Bedford County pioneer George Newman. Newman first came there in 1797 and, like many of his contemporaries, began life in that locale as a small farmer. However, he subsisted mainly by hunting both the small- and big-game animals that were so abundant at that time. Game was so plentiful in fact

---

1. Henry Wilson Storey, *History of Cambria County Pennsylvania, Volume 1*, 202.
2. W. J. McKnight, *Pioneer Outline History of Northwestern Pennsylvania*, 119.

Face of the wild. A grey wolf advancing through a dark woods—worst nightmare of a lonely nighttime traveler.

that it was not unusual for him "to provide a supply of meat for his family's morning meal by shooting a deer before breakfast."[3]

This was the way of the frontier, as was the isolation experienced by the family. They had few neighbors and the only sounds that broke the otherwise complete stillness of the dense forest that surrounded them were howls of ravenous packs of wolves, screams of prowling mountain lions, and guttural sounds of other savage beasts like scavenging black and brown bears.

There were no mills that were close by at that time, and so Mr. Newman, carrying his grain on his back, often had to walk fifteen miles to Fate's Mill near Cumberland to get his grist ground to meal or flour. It was on one such morning when Mr. Newman was not at home that members of his family were perplexed by an unusual succession of noises coming from the creek that coursed through the hollow in front of their rustic cabin.

Mrs. Newman and her oldest daughter Polly decided to investigate, and when they got down into the hollow and looked upstream, they saw a deer splashing and struggling in the water as it tried to escape from a panther that was chasing it. Upon seeing the mother and daughter the panther

3. Waterman and Watkins, *History of Bedford, Somerset, and Fulton Counties Pennsylvania*, 366–67.

gave up on its pursuit of the deer and rushed the frightened women, who managed to get back to the cabin and take refuge there.[4]

James Leasure, born in 1801, and his wife were natives of this same section of Bedford County, and they, too, passed on to their children and grandchildren tales of the panther and the wolf that they had experienced first-hand during their early days on the frontier. One of their favorites that has come down to the present day was about the time Mr. Leasure rescued a young neighbor lad from certain death by a pack of wolves determined to knock the boy off his horse. Michael Hillegass often told this story to his children and grandchildren as well, and it's from his account that the most graphic parts of the story are recalled.

Michael was also taking a trip to a mill that day, but he was on horseback. He had only gotten part way to the mill when he heard rustling sounds in the woods beside the bridle path and when he looked over, he saw a number of animals rushing toward him through the dark forest. At first, he thought it was dogs, but soon he realized that his pleasant uneventful horseback ride was turning into a nightmare, because the approaching beasts were wolves.

Two of the wolves attacked the boy and the horse, attempting to knock the boy to the ground. The attack badly frightened both the boy and his mount, but the level-headed lad managed to keep the horse under his control and spurred it on as fast as it would go toward the nearby home of James Leasure. The entire pack kept pace for a while, nipping and biting at the haunches and legs of the distraught horse, but eventually the horse outdistanced them, and the wolves turned and fled when they saw Mr. Leasure standing at his barn.[5]

This account is remarkably similar to a wolf attack preserved in that fascinating book by James E. Harting (published in 1880) titled *Extinct British Animals*. In his treatise Mr. Harting records an incident he verified as happening near Ballyroggin in County Kildare, Ireland, around 1725. His source was a seventy-year-old Irishman who had heard his father tell many wolf tales that were told to him by his grandmother. According to that esteemed Irish lass, born in 1731, she had been told the old wolf tales by her uncles, who actually were the ones who experienced the wolf encounters firsthand.

4. Ibid.
5. Ibid.

One of those uncles was a man named James Malone, and one of his favorite stories was the one about how his brother came galloping home on horseback one night with his horse in a lather because he was being chased by a pack of wolves. Before he could get home the wolves finally overtook him and his exhausted mount.

The frenzied pack continued to jump onto the hindquarters of the horse until the frightened rider caught a glimpse of his brother standing at their front door. Almost paralyzed with fear, young Malone could do nothing more than shout out to his sibling, "James, James, my horse is ate with wolves!" Upon seeing the other Malone brother standing at the ready, the wolves stopped, turned, and ran away.[6]

Further to the north in Warren County, about the same time as Michael Hillegass was having his wolf troubles in Bedford County, there was another pack of wolves which wanted to make a meal of another hapless man who encountered them on a nightly basis. Erastus Barnes was the son of Timothy Barnes, who is celebrated as the first settler in Sheffield Township of Warren County. Timothy was born in 1786 and came to Warren County around 1828 from Yates County, New York, settling along the south branch of Tionesta Creek where he built the first sawmill in that section.

Barnes had to cut his own roads into the area and the fourteen-mile journey from Warren to his mill site took four days. However, the dense forest made the location an ideal one for a lumber business since here Barnes found original lofty pine trees of unusually large size. One in particular seemed to be the granddaddy of them all, since its circumference was measured to be 23 feet at a height of eight feet up from the forest floor. It's also stated that yet another was so big that Barnes was able to saw it into seventeen saw-logs that were each sixteen feet in length.

The winter following the construction of his sawmill, Timothy Barnes went back to his family in New York State while his son Erastus stayed behind to work at a mill in Warren and to occasionally check on the workers at his father's mill as well. However, it turned out not to be a cushy family job nor one for the faint of heart.

Erastus always made the trip from Warren to his father's mill on foot and without any companions, and he was usually followed the entire way

6. James E. Harting, *Extinct British Animals*, 203–4.

A pack of wolves howling at the moon. Their unearthly chorus sent chills through the very hearts of settlers who shared the wilderness with them and heard their cries on a nightly basis.

by a pack of wolves. On one occasion it was getting dark by the time he spotted the workers' shanty in the fading light at the mill site, but although he was relieved to see it, he was also somewhat alarmed to find no one there. Apparently, the workers had all gone out on an extended hunting trip, and the only food left in the shanty was a spoonful or two of buckwheat and a small sliver of jerked venison.

Having no other options, the famished young overseer made a partial meal of the leftovers and spent a harrowing night in the rude hut surrounded by "hungry wolves howling about his ears in an ominous manner." The next day he made his way back to Warren only to find that the wolves had gotten back there before his arrival. It's not recalled as to how many days passed after this scary episode before young Erastus had the courage to make the solitary journey back to his father's mill once again.[7]

Both Erastus Barnes and Michael Hillegass would no doubt have counted themselves lucky when considering their narrow escapes from packs of wolves in full attack mode. On the other hand, they certainly would have considered themselves to have been divinely protected if they had ever been told of the fate of another man over in Perry County who wasn't as fortunate as them.

---

7. J. S. Schenck, *History of Warren County, Pennsylvania*, 513.

The episode in question was described in the *Burlington Free Press* during March of 1836, where it was reported that a wolf attack had occurred in Liberty Valley of Perry County, Pennsylvania, during that same month. The name of the man who was attacked by the wolves is not mentioned in the article and he is described as "an African-American worker who had spent a day helping neighbors butcher." That evening he apparently was returning home while "carrying portions of meat given to him as pay," and the fresh cuts of meat no doubt drew the pack of wolves to him.

When they finally attacked the tired and virtually defenseless man, he could only defend himself with a butcher knife he was carrying, but it was not enough. When they found his badly ripped and torn body the next day, they also found the carcasses of five wolves he had managed to kill with his knife before the pack killed him. After noting that that many dead wolves had been found beside the man, the paper further noted that "this led to speculation that the pack which attacked him had perhaps numbered a dozen or more."[8]

It might be conjectured that the unfortunate Perry County victim could have been able to save himself if he had been carrying a gun. At least that's what many would say, once they were told about a man that early settlers in Huntingdon County considered to be the ultimate frontiersman.

Perhaps it was because he always carried his trusty rifle with him no matter where he went that led his contemporaries to refer to him as a "mighty hunter." Whatever the reason, that's the title James McElroy eventually acquired and earned over the years, due to his many hunting exploits. There was one in particular, however, that probably secured his reputation as that mighty hunter. And this account told of the time where he almost wiped out a pack of ravenous wolves singlehandedly.

McElroy was making his way toward Huntingdon that day to pick up some provisions when a nice buck jumped out in front of him. The sudden appearance of the deer surprised him, and he only managed to wound it when he finally got his shot off. The deer took off running and McElroy started out in pursuit, knowing that it could not go far, judging from the blood trail it was leaving behind. Just as he expected, it wasn't long before McElroy saw the deer on the path ahead, but just as he was starting to size up his trophy, a large panther jumped out of the woods and onto the buck.

8. *Burlington Free Press*, March 1836.

Not willing to share his prize, McElroy raised his gun to shoot the panther, but initially could not get a good angle. Just as he thought he could take his shot, he heard a pack of snarling and whining wolves on the path behind him. By this time, it was nearly dark; and he was still a long way from home. Deciding it was best to first dispatch the panther, then deal with the wolves, he fired his gun and ended the beast's final meal. In desperation, he climbed the nearest tree and awaited the arrival of the noisy pack.

McElroy began shooting them one by one, which he continued to do throughout the night. Despite his deadly aim, the wolves were not scared away, probably kept there by the deer and panther meat they were devouring. However, when daylight finally came, the surviving wolves slunk back into the forest, leaving their fallen comrades behind.

At that point the tired mighty hunter crawled down from his perch in the tree and counted the wolves lying on the ground all around. When he was finished, he had counted "twenty-two dead wolves and a dead panther, the scalps of which he took to Huntingdon and drew a bounty of twelve dollars each."[9]

It was sizable bounty payments like this that in the end hastened the demise of the wolf packs in the state, as we saw in the previous chapter. Moreover, as also noted in the previous chapter, official bounty payment records seem to indicate that the last wolves were eliminated around 1884 or 1885 here in Pennsylvania. Despite the records, however, there were still reports of wolves in the more remote sections of our mountains, even as late as 1898.

It was reported in Mifflin County in that year, for example, that somewhere in the Seven Mountains "the beds of thirteen wolves had been seen that fall by some lumbermen." Most people, having not heard of wolves in the area for decades, dismissed the account, until it was reported in a Mifflin County newspaper shortly afterwards that a pack of wolves had attacked a schoolteacher in one of the adjoining counties."[10]

Similarly, old-time lumbermen Jared Ripka of Spring Mills, Centre County, born in 1885, told me he remembered of wolves being seen and heard in both Poe and Decker Valleys, two remote valleys of the northern Seven Mountains country, when he was a boy. He also recalled that

---

9. J. Simpson Africa, *History of Huntingdon and Blair Counties, Pennsylvania*, 265.
10. Samuel N. Rhoads, *Mammals of Pennsylvania and New Jersey*, 168.

sometime in the 1930s he and several others had just finished a day of butchering when they heard what they thought was the howl of a timber wolf on the mountain back of John Decker's old homestead in Decker Valley of Centre County.

So, could it mean that there were some wolf packs that survived well into the twentieth century in the Seven Mountains and in other similar remote areas of the state; survivors that constituted the most cunning members of the breeding stock? Even today, as coyotes become more plentiful throughout Pennsylvania, there are those who claim that Canadian wolves are drawn here to breed with their coyote cousins, while others say the coyotes interbreed with peoples' dogs, creating a new breed entirely which locals refer to as "coy dogs."

Since the Seven Mountains country of Centre and Mifflin Counties appears to have been one of the last strongholds of wolves in 1898 and perhaps later, it makes sense that coyotes still find the area attractive. An area of isolated beauty, the Seven Mountains and surrounding state forest lands yet today contain many acres of untouched miles to wander, state

A black wolf. Safely kept behind high sturdy fences at the Wolf Sanctuary in Lititz. Here you can hear a pack in full cry. It can still send chills up your spine even though you know the wolves are in pens!

parks, state game lands, and designated wild areas. And because it is so well preserved in a natural state, it remains an ideal spot for stealthy creatures like coyotes to settle into.

They have undoubtedly done so since locals in these spots hear the howls of coyote packs on a nightly basis. They are shy animals and aren't often seen, but every so often they can be spotted, just like the one my wife and I surprised one night when driving out of the depths of a remote valley in the foothills of the Seven Mountains.

It was a moonless night in 1994, while we were driving out of Decker Valley, when my wife spotted something along the road ahead. I slowed down and turned the truck's headlights onto the dark shape. The bushy-haired gray coyote, which looked to be about the size of a large German Shepherd, froze momentarily when the lights illuminated it, but then, with its long tail sticking straight out in back, it bounded easily up the side of the mountain like a silent phantom.

The idea that the animal may have been a wolf did not enter our minds, since we had heard reports of coyotes being seen in the area. Consequently, there are still many skeptics that remain doubtful that there are any wolves in Pennsylvania at all. Actually, there may be none, as there may only be coyotes and coy dogs. On the other hand, there may be some true wolves migrating into the state from Canada, drawn here by their coyote cousins. If this has happened, then it may be said that wolf days have once again returned to Pennsylvania.

CHAPTER VII

THE LAST PANTHERS

After the last packs of wolves had been exterminated in Pennsylvania, and lone wolves were a rarity as well, it wasn't too long before the Pennsylvania mountain lion met the same fate. At least that's what public opinion claimed was true, but if the demise of the Pennsylvania panther wasn't absolutely certain there were many people who certainly hoped that it was finally gone or soon would be.

The panther had been almost as much of a nuisance as the wolves had been, and to an individual traveling through a dark and lonesome woods at nightfall, its scream could be as frightening as a wolf's howl. One early settler in the Pennsylvania wilds had learned to live with the beast and to observe its habits, and he would later write: "They subsist entirely upon animal food, their usual prey being deer and rabbits. About the first of January is called the running season, being the time when they mate. When the first snows of winter come, they seek the rocky hills and sheltered places, where they remain until driven forth by hunger, when they frequently visit the farmyards of the settlers, and help themselves to any sheep or fowl that is within reach. From an Isrealitish antipathy to pork, or some other cause, they never attack a hog, passing by good fat ones to reach other animals."[1]

The following incident supports the old settler's claims, as it recalls one occurrence where a "half-grown panther" was caught stealing a farmer's stock, and it also describes just how dreadful the scream of the big cats could be. The panther in this case crept into a poultry-house along Pine Creek in Lycoming County one night and caused the chickens such alarm

---

1. Philip Tome, *Pioneer Life, or Thirty Years a Hunter*, 186.

that their loud cackling and clucking was heard by two women who were alone in the nearby farmhouse that night.

Supposing the henhouse intruder was a fox, they ventured forth carrying a gun and a lantern to light their way. Once at the scene of the disturbance they cautiously peeked inside the poultry-house and saw a large animal that they knew was not a fox. They were uncertain as to exactly what it was, and so, taking no chances, one of the brave maids shouldered the rifle and fired.

Immediately afterwards, the strange beast let forth a terrible scream that filled the women with such horror that they dropped the gun and their lantern and ran back to the house. Later, with their curiosity overwhelming their fear and when all was silent, they went back out again, only to find the beast lying dead on the poultry-house floor. Later, when the menfolk came home and saw that the women had shot a mountain lion, they declared that they were heroines of some note.[2]

Other accounts such as the preceding one are well documented, and together they prove without doubt that mountain lions would indeed attack livestock. Therefore, it's no wonder that the extermination of the big cats was looked upon as a positive goal by early agriculturalists. At first it must have seemed like an impossible task since the cries of the panther were so common and numerous both day and night; and had been since the first settlers ventured into the thick forests of the Pennsylvania wilderness.

Descendants of Aaron Hall, the great panther hunter of Unionville, Centre County, still can recall tales of how prevalent the panthers were said to have been in Hall's day. One account in particular also illustrates how bold the beasts could be. This event occurred one day when the menfolk were off hunting, and the womenfolk were at home preparing the evening meal. Their daily chores did not keep the women's minds off the howling of mountain lions that kept circling the barn and homestead, and they said they were frightened by them the entire day.

Likewise, the early settlers of Brush Valley, Centre County, would often have to watch out for panthers that were attracted to their maple sugar kettles when the sap was running in the maple trees in early spring. This alarming situation became less of a problem, however, after those same Brush Valley settlers built distilleries and used their Conestoga wagons to

---

2. Ibid.

Amanda Cornelia Ertel Gobble. Born in 1859,
she was the daughter of Samuel Ertel. See the
chapter titled "Sam Ertel's Panthers" in the author's
Pennsylvania Fireside Tales Volume 1 *for a tale*
about how, as just a small child, she became upset
one winter night when she saw a mountain lion
following her father across a snow-covered field.
(Photo courtesy of Mr. and Mrs. Robert Steiger.)

haul their whisky to Derrstown, as Lewisburg was called at the time, and trade their moonshine for refined white sugar.

Above all, however, it was the mountain lion's continuing appetite for the farmers' livestock that led to its eventual demise in Pennsylvania. Bounties were placed on its head, which increased the toll on its numbers, as did the use of the same techniques that had been used to exterminate the wolf. Such practices, of course, included the usually ineffective ring hunts as well as the use of dogs, which were often used with good success; at least if a statement by James Caldwell, an early settler in Noyes Township of Clinton County, can be regarded as factual.

Caldwell settled on Kettle Creek around 1800 and spent a lot of time in the woods either hunting or fishing. Plagued by the same beasts of prey as others living in that same wilderness, he finally decided to set up a large wolf pit to see if he could trap and kill the many wolves that made his life a constant torment.

To his dismay, however, the first three or four times he went to check to see if there were any wolves in his trap, he was surprised to find all his bait gone and no wolves in his pit. Finally, one day he decided to make a tour of inspection through the surrounding forest to see if he could find the thief that was robbing his trap, and he had not gone far before spotting a huge mountain lion resting comfortably under a rock ledge.

Unprepared to do battle with such a formidable foe, he made tracks for his cabin. Once there he grabbed his gun and his dogs, and also enlisted the help of as many of his neighbors as he could find. Once his posse was formed, he led them back to the place where he had seen the panther. The dogs soon picked up its track and were upon it in short order.

"A terrible battle ensued," Caldwell recalled, "and the dogs were soon worsted." Not intending to stand by and see what would happen, the old hunter, armed only with his hunting knife, ran at the panther, which, upon seeing his approach, broke away from the dogs and took off running. The pack pursued it with renewed courage and soon had it treed. Caldwell took his rifle and shot the panther, wounding it in the shoulder with his first shot, then shooting it in a vital spot the second time.

The dying mountain lion wrapped its long tail around the limb of the tree it was lying upon and determinedly hung on that way until it finally expired. After it fell to the ground the men measured its length and found it to be "eleven feet three inches from the tip of its nose to the end of its tail!" The men skinned and dressed the panther and later, upon eating the meat, they would declare that they had "never tasted better."[3]

Two trusty dogs also proved themselves to be useful companions when Samuel Snyder of Chapman Township, Clinton County, came across tracks of a large panther while out deer hunting after a good tracking snow had fallen in the winter of 1857. Never having shot one of the big game animals before, Snyder let his dogs start off at a run as they followed the beast's trail. The trail was fresh, and the dogs had no trouble following it for about two miles, at which point Snyder spotted a dead fox on the path ahead.

---

3. John Blair Linn, *History of Centre and Clinton Counties*, 648–49.

The wily fox had obviously been following the panther, probably hoping to feast off the mountain lion's kills after the panther had had its fill. But the panther, not in the mood for any such hindrances that might jeopardize its hunting success, had allowed the fox to approach just close enough that it could dispatch it with one swift stroke of its sharp-taloned paw.

On continuing on from there, it wasn't long before Snyder came upon the warm remains of a deer that the big cat had just killed. About twenty-five feet further, he heard both his dogs fiercely barking at something, but he could not see them since they had gone down a steep declivity in the trail ahead. Snyder ran ahead and peered down into the hollow where he saw a huge panther standing on the large trunk of a fallen tree. His dogs had hounded the beast until it had taken refuge there, and now it was growling and hissing at its tormentors.

The beast had no avenue of escape, so Snyder took a shot, only wounding the animal in the neck. It was not enough to kill the fierce brute, but the bullet enraged it so that it jumped to the ground and attacked the dogs, dealing one such a severe blow that it disabled it. The other dog was not deterred however and kept up the fight. This gave Snyder enough time to reload his rifle and administer a final fatal shot to the panther's head.

Snyder would later say that had his second shot not been effective the panther no doubt would have laid him and both his dogs low, so immense was its power. He noted also that he measured the big cat from the tip of its nose to the end of its tail and found it to be nine feet and two inches. Although Snyder was known for his physical endurance and courage, he would later say that while he stood looking down at the huge monster lying prostate at his feet after he had shot it, he "could not help but tremble at the thought of his imminent peril and thank God for his deliverance."[4]

Although a man could, in 1802, get twelve dollars bounty for killing a panther and another four dollars for the hide, and as much or more in later years, there were few hides sold. Instead, they were kept as trophies of the hunt, just as nice-sized sets of deer antlers were, and still are, often mounted and kept as proof of a hunter's prowess. Eventually, however, the hunting began to take its toll, and the number of panthers killed annually in Pennsylvania began to decline.

Then the lumber kings began to decimate the state's magnificent forests and the panther's food supplies shrunk as well. The combination of the two

---

4. Ibid, 585–86.

forces, diminished food supplies and relentless killing, finally brought an end the reign of the mountain lion as king of the Pennsylvania forests. It was at this point that official tallies of the "last panthers" were recorded in the records of County Courthouses, and which ran as follows:

1841—Last panther killed in Tioga County

1848—Last panther in Forest County killed at Panther Rocks

1851—Last panther killed in Cameron County (actually two panthers); killed by Isaac Rummage along the Driftwood Branch of Sinnemahoning Creek.

1857—Last Susquehanna County panther shot at Brushville by Samuel Brush.

1863—Last Warren County panther killed by Sylvester Williams in Corydon Township.

1869—Aaron Hall kills some of the last panthers in Centre County at Unionville along Rattlesnake Pike.

1872—Andrew Jackson Long shoots his last panther in Clearfield County.

Nonetheless, just like the reports about the "last wolves," accounts of the "last panthers" were not widely accepted. Many folks living in the wilderness of those times thought such claims to be greatly exaggerated, with some writers in 1905 beginning to raise the possibility that panthers might still be found in Pennsylvania's northern counties.

Others joined the chorus and began to put forth the idea that maybe the old saying that a panther was "harder to kill than a snake" was not such an exaggeration after all. It turns out that they may have been correct, at least if the following reports from recent years are to be believed:

1909: Cherry Run Kettle on Paddy Mountain (Snyder/Centre Counties):

Fred Malone shot a mountain lion here while deer hunting with John Seltzer in November. Upon measuring it they found that it stood two and a half feet high at the shoulder and was eight to nine feet long when its four-foot-long tail was included. Malone took his trophy home and neighbors from Coburn and surrounding towns flocked to see it until the men sent their trophy to the Department of Forests and Waters in Harrisburg to be mounted. It's not known what happened to it after that.[5]

1918: Thickhead Mountain Wild Area (Seven Mountains Centre County):

John Glascoe was hunting with a pack of hounds here when they treed a mountain lion. Glascoe shot it and dragged it back to what was then the Union Schoolhouse (now a hunting camp) along Boal Gap Road and hung it there on a large hemlock tree for public display. Measurements of its size have not come down to the present day, but descendants of those who saw it recall them saying that it was "a big one with a long tail."[6]

1926: Boal Gap (Detweiler Hollow, Centre County):

"Now when I was four years old my grandfather Franklin Treaster, he was a blacksmith, was shoein' a draft horse for my dad. I was always into some horses and so I was out here watchin'. Right over here in this direction, about halfway between here and the ridge, there's an animal went down through just cryin' like a baby! Of course that scared the britches off a little fella, you know, so I beat 'er to the house while my dad went down to get our neighbor Rube Colyer and his dog. So they went up and got on track of him, there was a tracking snow on the ground and they could see the tracks. They followed it west on Thickhead Mountain and over into Detweiler Hollow, that's the wildest country we've got around here, until it got dark. Rube Colyer said that it was a panther; he could see from the tracks. Now I actually heard it myself!"[7]

1949: Punxsutawney (Jefferson County):

"One of my boys told me, about three months ago, that he saw a big black animal, with a long tail that was pretty thick, in a field; and it was crying like a baby. I told him he was seeing things, but on the first day of rabbit season in Jefferson County, about 200 yards from my neighbor's barn. It was about five feet long with a thick tail and it seemed as though it had short legs and pointed ears, but I didn't hear it cry. I saw pictures of

---

5. Blaine Malone (born 1903), *The History of Coburn* (privately published), interviewed October 23, 1980 and April 21, 1981.

6. Vince Treaster (born 1922), recorded November 5, 1988.

7. Ibid.

panthers in *Pennsylvania Game News*, and it looked the same. Now in the 1948 *Game News*, Col. Henry W. Shoemaker had a story about the last panther killed in Pennsylvania. Now I think he's wrong!"[8]

1967: Venango Township (Crawford County):
A local hunter killed a small animal just outside Edinboro that was subsequently identified as a mountain lion. It weighed just 48 pounds and measured only five feet three inches from tip of nose to tip of tail; so, it was evidently a young one. A picture of the hunter and the lion, along with the District Game Protector, appeared in the *Pittsburgh Press* on November 5, 1967.

1972: Panther Hollow (Long Mountain, Centre and Mifflin Counties):
"I seen one in 1972, back on the road between Poe Valley and Poe Paddy—the road that comes up to the top of the mountain right up here where it comes out right at the head of Panther Hollow. The kids and I and my cousin and his kids were fishin' for brook trout. I'll never forget it! The sun was shinin' in my eyes, and it was evening. The sun was going down and it'd be right in your face, and I seen this big black cat goin' across the road.

"I said to the kids, 'Did you see anything?', and they said 'Yeah, it looked like a big black cat!' I said 'it looked to me like a panther," and the kid said 'Dad, I saw it too!'

"It just, zip—gone! I went home and called a friend of mine, works for the Game Commission, and I was tellin' him about it. He said 'What're you drinkin'!'"[9]

1985: First Mountain (Cumberland County):
During the winter of 1985 residents living along Wertzville Road heard screams coming from the top of First Mountain, and many were convinced they came from a mountain lion. Subsequent sightings appeared to prove them correct, and when the sightings persisted the State Game Commission came to investigate. They confirmed that at least one mountain lion, and perhaps two, had passed through here. They were thought to be wanderers from West Virginia or even from as far south as Louisiana, places where the big cats could still be found in the wilderness areas of those states.

---

8. Harris Breth, letter from radio personality "Smiling Steve" of Smoke Run, Pennsylvania.
9. Alvin Marquette (born 1943), recorded May 27, 1988.

An old logging sled pulled by teams of horses. Used to haul logs over snow covered log roads during the logging era. Displayed at the Thomas T. Taber Museum in Williamsport, along with many other fabulous relics of the West Branch Valley.

2023: Big Poe Mountain (Centre and Mifflin Counties):

In March of this year, a lone hiker sitting in his pickup truck, on the grounds of Hemlock Acres Campground just off the Millheim-Siglerville Pike, sees a large mountain lion standing on the edge of a field along the edge of the woods. It sizes him up, but apparently uninterested, just nonchalantly ambles away into the woods. His color photo captures a side view of the large cat with its long tawny-colored body, large head, and long black-tipped tail. The photo leaves no doubt that this was indeed a mountain lion. They are indeed here in our mountains, regardless of the denials of the Pennsylvania Game Commission![10]

Based on the small sampling of stories I've been able to collect over the years, it would appear that for the last hundred years the mountain lion has been making a slow comeback into the mountainous sections of Pennsylvania that were once its refuge. Much like the coyote, the animal the original settlers liked to call the panther seems to have learned to coexist with man in ways that allow it to adapt to modern conditions and to return to the forests it once ruled as king.

10. Mitchel Schaeffer, interviewed February 11–14, 2024.

CHAPTER VIII

END OF AN ERA

Although they were once very numerous in Pennsylvania, animals like the wolf, the mountain lion, and the elk eventually became extinct here in our mountains; their howls, screams, and bugles becoming only a memory in the minds of those who had once hunted them. And among those who witnessed and documented just how fast the decline of these animals occurred was a Scotch-Irish minister of the Church of England.

Joseph Doddridge, born in 1769, also studied medicine under Benjamin Rush in Philadelphia and his medical training provided a nice source of income as he traveled throughout the Pennsylvania frontier.[1] He kept careful notes during his travels and there was probably no man better qualified to report on the frontier than him.

In addition to his interactions with many frontiersmen in his capacity as a doctor and as a minister, Reverend Doddridge was raised in the Allegheny Mountains of western Pennsylvania when it was largely a wilderness. During his early youth he had helped his father clear trees for a homestead and had helped build a stockade in which he had sheltered beside his father while awaiting a war party attack during the perilous times of the Revolutionary War.[2]

He would write that he remembered his boyhood as being damp and chilly due to the dense dark forests. Summers were short and cool. Winters began early and lingered late, with deep snows and frosts lasting until May.

1. Joseph Doddridge, *Notes on the Settlement and Indian Wars*, 264.
2. Ibid, 222–24.

The old mountain homestead. This original log cabin was once the home of one of the earliest families to settle in the area. The Stovers lived in this one-room structure until they could afford a larger house, and then turned their original home into a summer kitchen. It still stands today along Green Grove Road near Spring Mills in Centre County.

However, he would also recall that as the forests were cut, he saw striking climactic changes occur during his lifetime, with warmer weather and winters that were less severe.[3]

Perhaps Doddridge's accounts amount to a strong warning about how mankind's disregard for his natural environment can lead to unintended consequences; a lesson that we today are perhaps learning, and in many cases denying, about climate change. With these changes there were others taking place as well that, although more subtle at first, would ensure that the forests and wildlife of Pennsylvania would never be the same again. It was to be the end of an era.

The shameful story of greed, waste, and total lack of conservation efforts is one that applies to both the way the lumber "kings" denuded Pennsylvania's forests and to the manner in which people annihilated many animal species that once lived in those same forests. Fortunately for us there were some farsighted individuals who took steps to preserve pockets

---

3. Ibid, 55–56.

Another view of the old mountain homestead.

of the grandeur that once was so typical of the Keystone State. It is in fact because of these few individuals that we have the state parks, state forests, natural areas, and wild areas that grace our land, and which are appreciated by all. In the case of some of the animals, however, help came too little and too late.

The early settlers here thought animals like the mountain lion and the wolf needed to be exterminated and conquered; much the same attitude they had about the vast forests that had to be cleared to get fields for planting crops. They justified both these prejudices on the grounds of survival; they needed food to eat, and wolves and mountain lions, or panthers as they typically called them, proved in their own efforts to survive, to be an economic hardship because of the damage they inflicted upon livestock. Farmers regularly lost chickens, cows, sheep, and pigs to these hungry predators, and so the husbandmen used every means they could think of to eliminate the problem.

As noted in previous chapters, their methods included poison, fire, grand hunts, ring hunts, and bounty payments. But bounties were at first not just paid on wolves and panthers, but also on other nuisance pests like squirrels and crows. Through the combination, then, of merciless hunting, even during breeding seasons, and rampant destruction of food sources, some of the state's finest game species were wiped out in the course of two hundred years. Moreover, it would appear that most of the damage was done during the last twenty-five years of the nineteenth century when lumbering operations were reaching their peak and the repeating rifle appeared on the scene.

In preceding chapters in this volume and in the other volumes of the *Pennsylvania Fireside Tales* series, there are many accounts of the last wolves, the last panthers, and the last elk that were killed in Pennsylvania. Similarly, there are other animals that once resided here that were just as interesting as the panther, the elk, and the wolf, but which were also wiped out by the dual conditions of thoughtless over-hunting and destruction of food supply, with the latter being the primary reason in almost all cases. Among these former creatures that once resided here but which were exterminated were unusual species like the white hare, the woods bison, the passenger pigeon, and the wild Pennsylvania Parrot or Carolina Parakeet.

There were some who claimed to have seen a white hare in Poe Valley of Centre County as late as 1915.[4] If so, it may have been the last of its kind in the entire state. The debate about the woods bison, on the other hand, centers on whether or not this larger cousin of the western prairie bison ever lived here at all. That has been an unsettled question for many over the years, especially since no convincing physical evidence of its presence here has ever been found and no firsthand eyewitness accounts appear in the historical record.

All proof of their existence here seems to be secondhand, mainly in place names that bear the signature title; names like Buffalo Run in Centre County and Buffalo Crossroads in Union County. Even then, there is evidence that early cartographers arbitrarily borrowed names from other maps, when an area on a map they were drawing had no local name associated with it.

On the other hand, there are secondhand historical accounts that do seem to indicate that there were such beasts here at one time; an example from present-day Clearfield County being one notable case. Moravian missionary John Ettwein traveled through here in the eighteenth century,

---

4. Clarence Musser (born 1884), interviewed August 28, 1971.

Woods bison today, reintroduced and thriving in the Alaska wilderness.

and in his journal entry for July 4, 1772, wrote "we came to Clearfield Creek, so called because on its banks there are acres of lands that resemble clearings, the buffalo that resort hither having destroyed every vestige of undergrowth, and left the face of the country as bare as though it had been cleared by the grub-axe of the pioneer."[5]

Today, however, there are those that say those cleared fields described by Ettwein were the result of the work of beavers who built many of their dams in the area. And so, this reference is suspect as well.

There is also historical evidence that seems to indicate that herds of woods bison may once have frequented neighboring states like New York, Maryland and West Virginia. Writing in his diary when passing through what is present-day Washington D. C., English navigator Samuel Argoll noted in 1612, "I found a great store of cattle as big as kine, of which, the Indians that were my guide, killed a couple, which we found to be very good and wholesome meate, and are very easy to be killed, in regard they are heavy, slow and not so wild as other beasts of the wilderness."[6]

Argoll's notes are not that convincing as far as what he actually saw, and it seems that there are no credible first-hand eyewitness accounts about the

5. John Blair Linn, *History of Centre and Clinton Counties*, 14.
6. Elaine C. Grandjean, "Buffalo in New York State," *The Conservationist—Magazine of New York State's Department of Environmental Conservation*, September-October 1982.

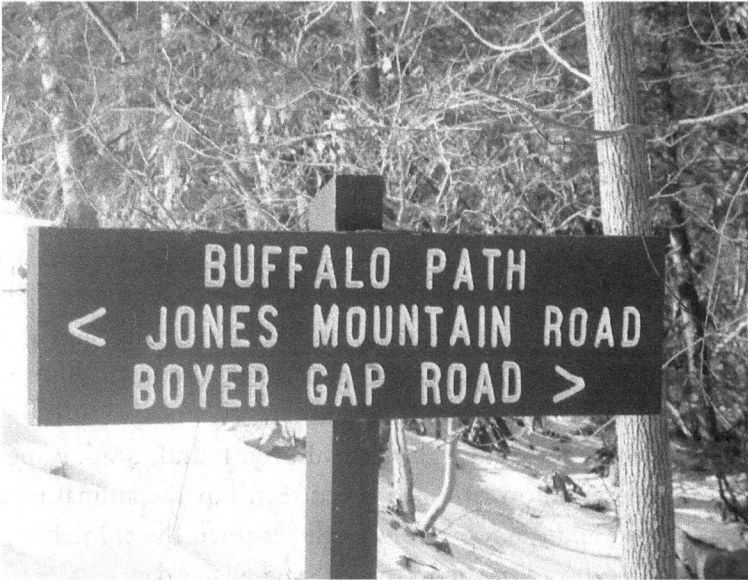

Sign at the Buffalo Path. Located along Route 192 near Rapid Run Hunting Camp in Union County, it marks the spot where the woods bison once trod. See the next chapter for details about this interesting part of Pennsylvania's storied past.

woods-bison being seen here in Pennsylvania either. However, there is one account I have found that may come as close to deciding the issue as any. Appearing in an 1876 issue of Harvard College's *Memoirs of the Museum of Comparative Zoology* there is a section titled "Occurrence of the Buffalo in Union County, Pennsylvania." Here J. A. Allen, the author, notes that he received a letter dated March 14, 1876, "from a professor J. R. Loomis of the University at Lewisburg, who writes:

'I have made inquiries as I could regarding the bison in this area. One man whose grandfather he well remembers, as well as much of his conversation, and who lived here one hundred years ago, never heard of the bison being native of this valley. Therefore, I went to see the oldest native-born citizen of this town, who is now 86 years old. He says there were no buffaloes in his early days, but it was a current notion in his boyhood days that there had formerly been.'"

In another letter, dated March 30, 1876, Professor Loomis wrote again:

"I have had a conversation with a Dr. Beck of this area, and he informs me that buffaloes, at an early day, were very abundant in this valley, and that the valley received its name from this circumstance. The doctor said he received his information directly from Colonel John Kelly three months before Kelly's death at age 88, in 1832. Kelly was a prominent and early settler in the valley and a soldier and officer in the Revolutionary War. He owned a farm about five miles from Lewisburg, in Kelly Township, which was named after him.

"Kelly told the Doctor that about 1790 or 1800 he was out with his gun on the McClister farm, which joined the farm of Colonel Kelly, and just at evening saw and shot a buffalo. His dog was young, and at so late an hour he did not allow it to pursue, and when he went to hunt for the buffalo the next morning, he could not find it. Nearly a week later, however, word was brought to him that it had been found, dead, some miles away. He found the information to be correct, but the animal had been considerably torn and eaten by wolves. He regarded the animal as a stray one and had never heard of any in the valley at a later day.

"The Colonel also told him that the valley was wooded originally with large but scattered trees, so that the grass grew abundantly and furnished good pasturage for the buffalo, and that from this circumstance they had once been very abundant in the valley. The Colonel said he had gotten this information from a friendly aborigine named Logan (probably not the chief of that name.) Dr. Beck also said he had the same statement from Michael Grove, also one of the first settlers in the valley."

Mr. Allen concludes his fascinating article by saying, "This, of course, affords satisfactory proof of the former existence of the buffalo in the region about Lewisburg, which forms the most easterly point to which the buffalo has been positively traced."[7]

There is one other account that is very compelling as well. British author Thomas Ashe came to America in 1806 with the sole purpose of exploring the western frontier. He traveled up and down the Ohio River, recording his thoughts and experiences along the way in the form of letters to himself, which are still regarded as some of the best accounts of what life was like west of the Appalachian Mountains at that time.

In one of those letters, he recalls a visit he had with an old settler in northwestern Pennsylvania who lived near Lake Erie. We include his

7. J. A. Allen, "Occurrence of the Buffalo in Union County, Pennsylvania," Harvard College's *Memoirs of the Museum of Comparative Zoology*, 1876.

The Buffalo Path. The way it looks today when entered at the Rapid Run Hunting Lodge along Route 192 in Union County. Obliterated long ago by logging operations, the deeply-trenched path was hollowed out by the hooves of countless woods bison that once used this route on their annual migrations across the mountains. See the chapter in this volume titled "End of an Era" for some interesting notes on this once-prevalent native of the state.

account in its entirety because of its interesting details and because it represents more testimony that supports the contention that there were indeed woods-bison here in Pennsylvania at one time.

"An old man, one of the first settlers in this country, built his log house on the immediate borders of a salt spring. He informed me that for the first several seasons the buffaloes paid him their visits with the utmost regularity; they traveled in single files always following each other at equal distances, forming droves on their arrival, of about three hundred each. The first and second years, so acquainted were these poor brutes with this man's house or with his nature, that in a few hours they rubbed the house completely down, taking delight in turning the logs of wood off with their horns, while he had some difficulty to escape from being trampled under their feet or crushed to death in his own ruins.

"In the first and second years this old man with some companions killed from six to seven hundred of these noble creatures, merely for the sake of the skins, which to them were worth only two shillings each, and after this 'work of death' they were obliged to leave the place till the following season, or till the wolves, bears, panthers, eagles, rooks, ravens, etc. had devoured the carcasses, and abandoned the place for other prey.

"In the following two years, the same persons killed great numbers out of the first droves that arrived, skinned them, and left the bodies exposed to the sun and air; but they soon had reason to repent of this; for the remaining droves, as they came up in succession, stopped, gazed on the mangled and putrid bodies, sorrowfully moaned or furiously lowed aloud, and returned instantly to the wilderness in an unusual run, without tasting their favorite spring or licking the impregnated earth, which was also once their most agreeable occupation; nor did they, or any of their race, ever revisit the neighborhood again."[8]

Ashe also noted that the old settler had told him that at the time when the bison rubbed down his house "he supposed that there could not have been less than ten thousand in the neighborhood of the spring." It must have been an amazing sight to see so many of these huge creatures traveling across the countryside, but when it's noted that such vast herds could be exterminated within several generations, it's not surprising that an even more abundant creature could be wiped out in Pennsylvania as well.

The Passenger Pigeon's demise is somewhat more perplexing however, given its even greater numbers. Huge flocks of pigeons could be seen during their annual migrations in the spring and the fall, and contemporary descriptions of them seem unbelievable today. In Forest County, for example, one historian noted that the flocks were accustomed to nest at Brookston every other year, and he went on to claim that "old settlers say that words almost fail to describe the vast numbers."[9]

Another historian in Warren County talked with one of the old men in the area who had once trapped the pigeons to make a living, selling the delicacy to eager buyers from near and far. That same old pigeoneer claimed to have seen "flocks at least one-quarter mile wide and about one-half mile long passing over Kane" and swore that the flocks of that size were not several flying one after another but one single flock that was "almost continuous."[10]

8. Thomas Ashe, *Travels in America Performed in 1806*, 47–48.
9. J. E. Henretta, *Kane and the Upper Allegheny*, 185.
10. Ibid, 187.

Similarly in Erie County another early settler described how flocks of Passenger Pigeons were sometimes drawn to the beechnut trees growing on his farmland, noting that some appeared to reach "from horizon to horizon" so vast were their numbers.[11]

Although not as numerous as the Passenger Pigeon, numbers of the colorful Carolina Parakeet once flew though our forests as well, and the size of their flocks could be as small as one hundred or as large as a thousand birds. In this case, however, it was not so much their numbers or their brilliant plumage that was their defining characteristic as much as the destruction they caused to crops.

They were particularly noted for their wanton destruction of orchards, which they would descend upon, knocking fruit off the trees without even so much as tasting it. The birds would also feed on stacks of grain and on corn shocks, leaving few kernels for the farmers. As a result, the agriculturalists used every means possible, including cats, shotguns, and wooden clubs, to kill as many of the parrots as they could.

Using almost the same methods they used against parrots, people also used nets against the Passenger pigeon, which were found to be a much more effective way to capture them. Unlike the Carolina Parakeet, pigeons were killed more for their value as a culinary delicacy rather than as pests that were an economic liability. Parrots, on the other hand, hit the farmer where it hurt most—his pocketbook. It could be said then that the extermination of both birds was, once again, due to relentless slaughter, elimination of their food supplies, or a combination of both.

In the case of the Passenger Pigeon, once the virgin forests of Pennsylvania's Black Forest were gone, felled by the lumberman's axes and saws, beech trees that once grew there in profusion disappeared as well. Beech nuts from those trees had been the primary food supply for the Passenger Pigeons, and after they were gone the birds that had depended upon them died out as well.

Much like today, economic factors always seem to keep surfacing when the reasons behind the extinction of an animal species, including all those we mentioned, are analyzed. Panthers and wolves killed livestock, Carolina

---

11. Betty Bechtel, "John Hamilton, Part I: Chronicler of the 19th Century," State College, PA, *Town and Gown Magazine*, August, 1981.

Parakeets damaged crops, while Passenger Pigeons, elk, and woods bison served as valuable food sources. Although intense efforts caused the decline of these creatures initially, it really wasn't until the large forests, and the food supplies they supported, were gone, that the animals' fate was finally sealed.

Once again, however, it was the money to be gained from the trees themselves that led men to cut them down. As a result, the animals suffered two-fold. Not only did they lose their habitat and food supplies, but some were also sought after as a food source for the hungry lumber crews, or woods hicks, that were cutting down those same trees.

There were very few farms in the northern forests in that day, and so there was no ready source of beef, milk, and eggs to feed hungry workers. In order to at least remedy the scarcity of meat, the lumber companies turned to those men who made their living killing wolves and mountain

A link to days gone by. A skilled taxidermist preserved this bobcat's body for display at Greenwood Furnace State Park in Huntingdon County, where it can be seen today. The little cat with its black-tufted ears and "bobbed" tail serves as a reminder of the animals that even today still call our forests home. But it is also a reminder of the times when the wolf, the mountain lion and the elk also roamed these same forests and made the woods come alive with their stentorian cries.

lions and collecting the bounties on them. These "professional hunters" or "market hunters" were then offered even more money to provide bear, deer, and elk meat to the lumber camps, and they contracted with the lumber companies to bring in a given amount per week.

One rule often written into their contracts was that they could only provide bear meat once per week since it often had a rank flavor. Venison was the standard fare, with elk meat providing some variety, and so the numbers of deer and elk killed by individual hunters seems amazing when old records are read. Consequently, it is the exploits of some these professional hunters that form a unique chapter in the history of our state. Their adventures are set down in this and other volumes of the *Pennsylvania Fireside Tales* series, and it seems safe to say that today there are no hunters who are as rugged and fearless as some of those of times past.

Perhaps the rigors of those days called for tougher men, or perhaps the abundance of animals like the panther and the wolf inspired men to be tougher. Whatever the case may be, we can only look back today in wonder and disbelief. Times and men like these will probably never come again, and perhaps we all lack something because of that.

These men and their stories come from a wild and romantic chapter of Pennsylvania's past that was unique. It was unique not only in terms of ecological conditions but also in terms of lifestyle, morals, and ethics. Although there were many things that today appear wrong to us about their decisions and attitudes, we are in no position to criticize them, since we are, in many cases, so far away from the best parts of that culture that we need to slow down, look back, and try to see what we've lost.

If we don't do so, we'll end up continuing on our present path of reducing life to nothing more than a series of debits and credits, with no appreciation for the simpler things of life; things like the soft whisper of the wind in the trees, the colors of a flaming sky at the "golden hour," a majestic view from a wind-blown mountain top, or the cries of the wilderness which, even today in Pennsylvania, may resonate with the howl of the wolf or the cry of the mountain lion. Perhaps if we slow down long enough to look and to listen, we'll find that the wild and romantic era of Pennsylvania's storied past never ended at all; that it was only resting until it could surface once more.

Joseph Doddridge's original homestead. Thought to be one of the first dwellings built in Independence Township of Washington County, Pennsylvania, it was still standing when photographed in 1911. Also known as Doddridge's Fort, it was built by Joseph Doddridge in 1773 to serve as a refuge for settlers from Indian attacks. (Photo from the 1912 first edition of Doddrige's Notes.)

NOTES:

1. Comments on the woods bison of Pennsylvania would not be complete without further discussion on the controversy over whether it was ever resident in our state or not. The last verdict on that seems to have come from John E. Guilday, whose article titled "Evidence for Buffalo In Prehistoric Pennsylvania" appeared in the *Pennsylvania Archeologist* magazine of September 1963 (see volume #33-3).

In his abstract Guilday states the following: "Neither archeological finds nor trustworthy historical references can be used to prove or disprove the occurrence of bison in Pennsylvania in prehistoric times or during the Eighteenth Century. Reported buffalo bones are from sites which produced bones of domestic animals and may have been cow bones. Most circumstantial accounts of buffalo in western Pennsylvania turn out to be based on the doubtfully authentic statements of Thomas Ashe (1808). Place names and fairly abundant traditional stories do, however, suggest that the bison was present in the late Eighteenth Century, in small numbers."

Guilday dismisses Thomas Ashe's accounts as being in the same vein as that of Henry W. Shoemaker, who also wrote some anecdotes about the woods bison in Pennsylvania, but which appear to be, in part, based on Ashe's accounts (see in particular Shoemaker's "A Pennsylvania Bison Hunt," and compare it with Ashe's description of how bison herds in Erie County knocked down a settler's log cabin there).

Guilday notes that both men were prone to "colorful embellishment without regards to facts," noting in particular Ashe's descriptions of bears with five-inch tusks and twelve–foot rattlesnakes he encountered in his Pennsylvania travels. Nonetheless, Guilday does leave open the possibility that the bison was present here in small numbers at one time. Surprisingly he does not support his conclusion with any reference to J. A. Allen's 1876 article about Colonel John Kelly's account of the woods-bison in Union County. It seems that this still remains the best evidence on the matter.

2. Along with the many other species that have declined, or which have been exterminated altogether in our state, we have to include the rattle-snake as well. As one Juniata County historian has noted, "Older newspapers indicate that snakes in the olden times were not only more numerous, but also considerably larger and more vicious than their twentieth century descendants."[12] He supports his statement by then describing several six-foot long blacksnakes being killed in the Juniata Valley, and also the killing of several large rattlesnakes there, one with 11 rattles and another 'that had fifteen rattles that Amos Zook killed while huckleberrying."[13] See the chapter titled "Rattlesnake Rock" in the author's *Pennsylvania Mountain Landmarks Volume III* for more interesting accounts of this once-numerous reptile.

---

12. S. Duane Kauffman, *Mifflin County Amish and Mennonite Story*, 206.
13. Ibid.

CHAPTER IX

PENNSYLVANIA'S BOYS
IN BLUE

There have been countless histories written about that great American conflict known as the Civil War, and it might be thought that by now the topic has been researched and analyzed to the point where no further new material could be obtained. However, much to my surprise, I have, over the last several years, been often approached by individuals who are eager to share stories of their family heroes; Union soldiers whose personal experiences during the Civil War have never been recorded on the printed page. In this chapter I want to share some of those tales, not only to preserve them but also to honor the men who lived them—those who wore the blue uniform of the Union soldier and, as a result, were sometimes called Pennsylvania's Boys in Blue.

MARCHING TO THE BEAT OF A DIFFERENT DRUM

Joshua Snook, born in 1849, was just 14 years old when he enlisted in Battery C and F of Captain James Thompson's Pennsylvania Light Artillery Brigade. Born in Yeagertown, Mifflin County, the young farm boy's parents may have been subsequently relieved to learn that their son was to be the unit's drummer boy, but their relief was not warranted.

It was true that a unit's drummers and buglers were considered noncombatants; they did not carry muskets or other weapons, and they usually moved to the rear when fighting began. On the other hand, drum and

Thompson's Pennsylvania Battery C and F Monument. Gettysburg Battlefield Artillery Monument.

bugle calls were a way for commanders to issue commands during a battle, and there was no safe haven for anyone, including drummers, who sometimes were killed during a battle.

One notable example of this being the case was the fate of the drummer boy for Company F of the 49th Pennsylvania, Army of the Potomac VI Corps. Charley King was just 13 years old when he enlisted in 1861, but by 1862 he was already a veteran, having survived through the Peninsula Campaign in early 1862. Then in late 1862, his regiment was pursuing Robert E. Lee's army and had just had a minor skirmish, before arriving at the outskirts of Sharpsburg, Maryland on September 17. The regiment was waiting in a rear staging area in the East Woods near Miller's cornfield when a stray Rebel shell exploded over them, sending a hail of shrapnel down on the heads of the defenseless Yanks.

One piece of the jagged metal pierced King in the chest as it whirled down from the sky, severely wounding the young drummer boy. He was immediately taken to a field hospital where he died three days later. He holds the distinction of being the youngest casualty of all those that died during that terrible battle and perhaps during the entire Civil War.

Today, it is its level of casualties, a combined tally of almost 23,000 dead, wounded, or missing, that still ranks the Battle of Antietam as the bloodiest single day in United States history. To this day King is known to be the youngest soldier, of either Union or Confederate armies, to have been killed in action during the Civil War. His burial place has never been found, since he may have been buried in a mass grave along with others killed at Antietam. However, a monument to his memory can be found in Green Mount Cemetery at his hometown of West Chester, Chester County, Pennsylvania.[1]

Drummer boy Charlie King enlisted at age 12, killed in battle at age 14.

Joshua Snook was a little luckier than Charley King. Before and after Snook's short time with Thompson's Battery, the unit took part in many notable engagements from June 3, 1863, to March 25th, 1864, including Rappahannock Station, Cedar Mountain, Crooked Run, Thoroughfare Gap, Second Bull Run, Chantilly, Antietam, Fredericksburg, Purdy's Dam, Chancellorsville, Gettysburg, Mitchell's Ford, Mine Run, and Morton's Ford. Nonetheless, it was at Gettysburg where Snook's luck ran out.

Amidst that awful scene of carnage, a Confederate sharpshooter took aim and fired at a drummer boy he had picked out as his target. His Minié ball found its mark, hitting Joshua in the knee. Crumpling to the ground and unable to get up, Joshua was at first taken for dead and was thrown atop a pile of corpses. But an alert surgeon, perhaps hearing the boy's moans, discovered he was still alive and dragged the groaning lad off the pile.

Upon examining the teen's shattered knee, the surgeon realized he probably had no option except an amputation, but he also knew that an amputation under battlefield conditions usually was as good as a death sentence. After a brief discussion, the surgeon and his officers decided not to amputate, but to place Snook on a horse and send him off to Harrisburg with a message for Union headquarters there.

---

1. https://www.findagrave.com/memorial/7553200.

Charlie King's grave and memorial gravestone, located in West Chester cemetery, West Chester County, Pennsylvania.

It was a risky gamble, not knowing if the tough young man could remain conscious long enough to guide the horse to the state capital, let alone survive the trip at all. They figured if they tied him to the horse, he at least would have a fighting chance of staying alive, and their gamble paid off. Young Snook did survive the odds, making it to Harrisburg where doctors managed to save his leg and nurse him back to health.

Too crippled after that to be able to return to active duty, Joshua went back to Yeagertown, where he worked as a grave digger at the cemetery for many years. However, during those years when he should have been able to enjoy some peace and to be honored as a hero in the eyes of his contemporaries, he did not find that it played out that way at all.

Joshua's war wound made him a cripple for the remainder of his days. His bad leg meant he had to limp along with the aid of a cane in his old age, and ill-mannered local youths would taunt him about it. This disrespect infuriated the old soldier, and he would try to strike the rude youths with his cane. It was a counterproductive action since this belligerent behavior led to his being called "Crazy Joe" by many locals.

Snook died in Yeagertown and is buried in the same cemetery where he dug the last resting places of those who he now counts as his interred

Injured soldiers at Spotsylvania in May of 1864. A scene familiar to Chaplain William Henry Stevens.

neighbors. Nevertheless, his memory lives on, and he has received the honor and respect he deserves; from his descendants, who continually pass on his story to their children and grandchildren, and by the state of Pennsylvania, that placed his name on the Pennsylvania Monument at Gettysburg.[2]

Additional color and details surrounding the story of Joshua Snook and his fellow Civil War drummer boys are probably best preserved in the book titled *Recollections of a Drummer Boy*. Written by Harry M. Kieffer, a drummer boy from Mifflinburg in Union County, who was 16 when he enlisted in the Union Army in 1862, it contains descriptions of some of the same sights that Joshua Snook must have seen after being wounded at Gettysburg. In his book, Kieffer recalls that on the evening of July 5th, the second day after the battle of Gettysburg ended, he and a comrade "took our way across the breastworks, stone fences, and redoubts to look over the battlefield." He was not prepared for what he was about to see.

2. Nick Snook, interviewed August 19, 2018.

"I had frequently seen pictures of battlefields, and had often read about them," he wrote, "but the most terrible scenes of carnage my boyish imagination had ever figured fell short of the dreadful reality as I beheld it after the great battle of the war. Dismounted gun carriages, shattered caissons, knapsacks, haversacks, muskets, bayonets, accoutrements, scattered over the field in wildest confusion, —horses, poor creatures! Dead and dying, —and worst and most awful of all, dead men by the hundreds! I sicken of the dreadful scene, can endure it no longer. It's too awful to look at anymore! And so we go back to our place in the breastworks with sad, heavy hearts, and wonder how we could have ever imagined war so grand and gallant a thing when, after all, it is so horridly wicked and cruel."[3]

BIG FEET AND LITTLE SHOES

Casper Fisher, born in 1824, was just the kind of man the Union army was hoping to find. He stood six foot six and weighed in at 260 pounds. He more than likely would have made an ideal professional football player in any of today's leagues because along with his bulk he was also reputed to be extremely strong. One story that illustrates his strength, and which was often recalled about him, tells of the time when he was driving his buggy home from Huntingdon to Entriken, Huntingdon County, beside the tracks of the Broad Top Railroad.

After rattling along for a while he looked up and saw two men struggling unsuccessfully to get a railroad handcar back on the tracks. Fisher stopped and watched as they pushed and shoved and strained to lift it up without moving the heavy conveyance more than a few inches. Finally, having seen enough, he jumped out of his buggy, walked over to the handcar, and much to the surprise and delight of the track workers, singlehandedly lifted it up onto the steel rails.

It's not known when Fisher's feat of handcar strength occurred, but most likely it happened sometime prior to the start of the Civil War. When that war finally started, Fisher was 37 and still living in Entriken with his wife Margaret and their three daughters. Not only had his family grown but he may have as well, because by the time he went off to war his feet were so big that he wore a size thirteen shoe. That's fairly big even by today's standards, but back then it was almost unheard of. It was so atypical that

---

3. Harry M. Kieffer, *Recollections of a Drummer Boy*, 121–23.

Uncle Sam had to have special shoes made for the new recruit.

The new shoes apparently lasted for some time, because Fisher eventually did fight in several battles throughout the war along with his fellow soldiers in Company K, 78th Regiment Pennsylvania Volunteers. That regiment served valiantly throughout the war, fighting in engagements like the Battle of Stones River, Chickamauga, Chattanooga, and Missionary Ridge. Eventually, with all that marching and fighting, Casper Fisher's big boots did finally wear out and, unable at that point to provide him with new boots of the same size, the army had no choice but to honorably discharge him.

Lt. Col. Archibald Blakeley, 78th Pennsylvania Infantry.

After releasing him from service, the army placed him on a train that took him back to Huntingdon. It was up to him as to how he was going to get back home to Entriken, and his only choice was to walk. He had no shoes but started out anyway, traveling the entire distance barefooted. The time required to make that painful trek is not known anymore, but Fisher did make it back to his beloved home, and there he remained until he died. He's buried in the White Church Cemetery at Old Jacobs Church, Hesston, Huntingdon County.[4]

Huntingdon County soldier Casper Fisher was not the only Civil War recruit who had difficulties getting the right sized shoes and uniform. Apparently, it was a fairly common problem, and one which was colorfully recalled by another Pennsylvania veteran of the Civil War in his classic account of his time with Company D, 150th Pennsylvania Volunteers. The 150th was a Pennsylvania Bucktail Regiment mustered into service at Camp Curtin in Harrisburg during the fall of 1862. It was here at the Quartermaster Department that the new recruits got their Union uniforms and marching boots, and their first taste of army life.

It was a process that the new recruits would never forget and, in his reminiscences, one of them would later say that there were "so many men to be uniformed and so little time to do it," that "the blue clothes were

---

4. Robert Grace (great-great-grandson of Casper Fisher), interviewed July 18, 2012.

passed out to us almost regardless of the size and weight of the prospective wearer."

"With our clothes on our arms," he continued, "we marched back to our tents, and there proceeded to get on the inside of our new uniforms. The result in most cases was astonishing! For, as might have been expected, scarcely one man in ten was fitted."[5]

His account continues with descriptions of how humorous some of his ill-fitted comrades looked in hats too small or pantaloons that looked like knee-breeches on some or that were six inches too long on others. With a little trading the men got themselves fitted out with their correct sizes, but it was the footwear that was a problem not so easily resolved.

"And the shoes!" he exclaimed, "Coarse, broad-soled, low-heeled "gunboats," as we afterwards learned to call them—what a time there was getting into them! Here came one fellow down the street with shoes so big that they could scarcely be kept on his feet, while over yonder another tugged and pulled and kicked himself red in the face over a pair that would not go on."[6]

He also mentions a rumor that gained wide circulation around the Union camps concerning another soldier and his shoes. The soldier, in a different company, was said to be "a great strapping six-footer, who could not be suited," and with feet so big that "the largest shoe furnished by the government was quite too small." Like a good soldier the giant of a man tried his best to squeeze his feet into the boots, but at last he gave up, making him the object of the laughter and jests of his comrades. The big man took it in his stride and after a few minutes of the teasing finally exclaimed, "Why, you don't think they are all boys that come to the army, do you? A man like me needs a man's shoe, not a baby's!"[7]

It's a remarkable account that makes it hard not to think that the "great strapping six-footer" in this story was none other than big-footed Casper Fisher from Entriken.

FOOTLOOSE BUT NOT FANCY FREE

At the Battle of Cross Keys in the Shenandoah Valley of Virginia on June 8, 1862, and during Confederate General Stonewall Jackson's Valley

---

5. Harry M. Kieffer, *Recollections of a Drummer Boy*, 121–23.
6. Ibid.
7. Ibid.

Campaign, the 27th Pennsylvania often found themselves in the thick of the fighting. Bullets and cannonballs flew thick and heavy through the smoke-filled battlefield that day, and many soldiers ended up as casualties of the deadly swarm of lead. One casualty in particular would stick in the minds of his commanding officers after he had taken a Rebel bullet through his cheek. "By the Lord, I can't stand this!" was the man's lament after receiving his wound. "Why a fella isn't safe of his life here!"[8]

There were many who would have agreed, and all who experienced the horror of any Civil War battle would recall the dread that preceded it, the intensity of it, and the horror that often followed. As one poetic man described his feelings when he was about to go into battle; "There was silence deep as death, and the boldest held his breath."[9]

William Henry Stevens, one of the chaplains of the 148th Pennsylvania, knew these passions of war better than anyone, since his duty was to minister to the wounded and dying, in the many field hospitals that sprang up like bad weeds during and after a battle. Here he spent much of his time trying to console those who had been severely maimed and torn apart, and he may have, in the years following the war, suffered from the typical veteran malady we today call Post Traumatic Stress Syndrome (PTSS).

It would have been a miracle if he had not fallen victim to that psychological effect, and if he did, one of the incidents contributing to that affliction may have occurred after the hellish struggle at Po River on May 8, 1864. The night after the battle ended, Chaplain Stevens found himself ministering to several hundred wounded men, having the assistance of only one weary soldier who had been detailed to assist him.

The compassionate chaplain could see how exhausted the man was and, knowing he had been in battle all day and that he would no doubt have to fight the next, told him to take his blanket and lie down to get some rest, saying he would wake him later. He let the soldier sleep all night and let him go the next morning, even though Stevens had been up all night himself.

He had carried water from a distant spring at the foot of a nearby hill the entire night so he would have enough to slake the thirst of his wounded charges and have an ample supply to keep their bandages wet.

---

8. Commonwealth of Pennsylvania, *Pennsylvania at Chickamauga and Chattanooga*, 64.
9. Ibid, 215.

Burying the dead at Spotsylvania.

The black-as-ink little spring sat in an eerie and dismal glen surrounded by tall pine trees in which many owls liked to roost, and all night long he was serenaded with their melancholy cries. He would later recall that night many times, saying it was the most nerve-racking one he had ever had to endure. To his dying day he would aver that he wasn't sure which was worse, "the moans of the suffering in the hospital" or the "hooting of the owls in the pines over the spring."

It proved to be an awful night for the chaplain since by the time morning came, he had ushered eighteen souls into the next world. And his night shift was filled with the moans and groans of the wounded and dying. Of those eighteen men who did die, the chaplain would poignantly tell of one who had been shot through the heel and was suffering excruciating pain.

The wounded man groaned in agony without ceasing until finally the man beside him pleaded with him: "Comrade cannot you keep quiet? I cannot sleep and do not care to, but perhaps some of the boys could if we were quiet."

The groaning man ceased his cries long enough to reply that "I cannot; I suffer so with my feet!"

To which the other man replied, "I have both feet off!"

To the surprise of the chaplain, "the former died, the latter lived." The chaplain found another soldier who was inconsolable because he had lost one of his feet. He pointed out to the man that he was surely going to be discharged and sent home since he could fight no more.

But the disconsolate warrior burst into tears and exclaimed "But Chaplain, what will my poor wife and children do now that I am not able to provide for them?" The chaplain could only muse later that "this was a hard question to answer in those days."[10]

It was also presumably a question that men, like Casper Fisher, who had trouble fitting into their shoes on the day their uniforms were issued would pray they would never have to ask. Nevertheless, the horrible memories of war could, even in the old veterans' remaining years, never be erased from their minds. Along with the stress-inducing thunder of artillery bombardments and the rattle of musket fire shattering the stillness of the night, with the flashes sparkling in the darkness, a man's nerves would often be frayed to the breaking point and would never be the same.

SWEARING THEM IN

Two months after the Battle of Gettysburg, Union and Confederate forces once again clashed in another great battle that would result in a number of casualties that was second highest following their terrible three-day engagement in Pennsylvania. On September 18th, 1863, Union Major General William Rosecrans and his Army of the Cumberland met Confederate General's Braxton Bragg's Army of Tennessee near a small creek in northwest Georgia, just about three and a half miles outside the strategically important town of Chattanooga.

If some historians are to be believed (and there is debate about the authenticity of this translation), the name of the creek from which the battle was to receive its name can be translated from the Cherokee as "River of Death." Some attribute the Cherokee's choice of name to early warfare; assuming that one of their greatest battles must have taken place here, resulting in so many casualties that the creek flowed red with blood.

However, others say the Cherokee name came from the fact that it was here that many of their number contracted smallpox and subsequently died. Others translate the name in a different way, but regardless of the true translation, "River of Death" is a title that is no longer unreasonable.

---

10. J. W. Muffly, *The Story of Our Regiment—A History of the 148th Pennsylvania Volunteers*, 198–99.

Casper Fisher's last resting place. White Church Cemetery at Old Jacobs Church, just outside Hesston, Huntingdon County (photo taken by the author in 2019).

The Civil War Battle of Chickamauga in September of 1863 may not have resulted in a veritable "river of death," but considering the casualty count it could certainly have looked like a sea of blood when the guns finally fell silent. Typical of many such battles of that war, the Battle of Chickamauga oftentimes saw confusion reign supreme amidst the shouts and curses of men, roar of cannons, and bursts of musket fire.

One such incident was documented by Lieutenant Colonel Archibald Blakeley when recalling how his 78th Pennsylvanians "struck the cedar thickets near the Chickamauga." He was "riding an active, strong, young horse" at the time, and "in the confusion felt the horse give way, and supposing him to have been shot, I sprang from him, giving entire attention to getting the regiment into line."

Caught up in the intensity and confusion of the moment, the young officer "was astonished to find myself swearing at the top of my voice, which amazed me as I deprecated it and had forbidden swearing." He was overheard by one of his B Company lieutenants, whose "quizzical look" he was never to forget. But it was Lieutenant Mechling's comment that also stayed with him until the day he died.

"All right, Colonel, but you'd a never got 'em in line if you hadn't swore 'em in," was the tongue in cheek jab proffered by the young lieutenant, although he could have just as well said something along the lines that the situation was enough "to make a preacher swear." A comment like that was one that may have often entered the thoughts of the chaplain for the 148th Pennsylvania whose story was set down in the previous tale.[11]

---

11. Commonwealth of Pennsylvania, *Pennsylvania at Chickamauga and Chattanooga*, 219.

CHAPTER X

A DARK AND BLOODY GROUND

When historians wrote about the many border wars that were fought here in Pennsylvania and in other states during the colonial period, they often referred to those areas as "dark and bloody grounds" due to the quantity of blood, settlers' and aborigines' alike, that stained the very earth on which those battles were fought. In Pennsylvania, the records of those events have been preserved in the state's Colonial Records and in other works like C. Hale Sipe's *Indian Wars of Pennsylvania* and Loudon's *Indian Narratives*. They've also been preserved in oral histories that have been passed down through generations of descendants of those who fought in those border wars.

The following narratives are from these very same sources that describe those dark days in Pennsylvania's history, and at first it may seem like they are one-sided; included here just to cast the Native American in an unfavorable light. However, that is not the author's intention, since he has emphasized in his previous volumes of the *Pennsylvania Fireside Tales* series that he is on the side of Pennsylvania's aboriginal population when it comes to their claims of mistreatment at the hands of colonial authorities.

There is no question that Pennsylvania aborigines were mistreated, cheated, shamefully displaced from their homes and homelands, and disrespected by European colonists in deplorable fashion. It is an indelible black mark on the settlers who forged into the Pennsylvania frontier to carve out their homesteads from the dense forests that the natives revered.

The Harmony Inn, Harmony, Butler County. Not only is it an excellent place to eat and a seat of warm hospitality, but the inn is also thought to be one of the most haunted in Pennsylvania. Midway between here and Evans City a small Lenni Lenape Indian village once grew up along the Connoquenessing and Breakneck creeks, and along the Venango Indian Path, which ran through what was then the Ohio Country during the French and Indian War. During that time it was given the name Murdering Town, possibly by George Washington or his companion George Gist who were fired upon here by a lone Indian. The bullet missed, but had it killed Washington this area would have indeed become a hallowed part of Pennsylvania's "dark and bloody ground."

The Pennsylvania border war narratives that follow, and others that have appeared in numerous chapters in my *Pennsylvania Fireside Tales* books, will no doubt lead some readers to think that Pennsylvania's Native Americans were inferior to the colonial settlers in many ways. This even became clearer to me after being invited to address several writing classes at Lock Haven University.

The students had been asked to read at least one of my books before I came, and after I had spoken to one class and opened the floor up to questions, one brave young lady raised her hand and said that in my chapters touching on Pennsylvania's Indians and the wars with them, it seemed like I was "Indian bashing."

The question took me somewhat by surprise momentarily, but then I said to her that I could understand how she might reach that conclusion. I noted that the historical references I used in my stories came from histories written in the nineteenth century when historians' biases were still on the side of European settlers. They still at that time had the inclination to believe that aborigines were nothing more than uncultured ruthless barbarians, and their writing reflected that.

However, over the years it's been realized that winners of wars write the history of those wars in ways that reflect best on them, and it was no doubt the same in this case. It was, in fact, not until the latter part of the twentieth century that historians began to look at things from the Indians' perspective and began to realize that past writing had been a bit skewed.

So, with those thoughts in mind we'll continue on and introduce the reader to some of the more unusual human-interest stories that came from Pennsylvania's days of border warfare. These anecdotes can be unnerving and somewhat gruesome in many cases, but they reflect the reality of those times.

The reader should also keep in mind that frontier fighters often committed atrocities of their own when it came to fighting savage warriors. As such, then, the tales that follow can be thought of as biased pen pictures, but in a more fanciful way they can also be thought of as seedlings that sprouted from the fields that once comprised Pennsylvania's own "dark and bloody ground."

A TREASURE FOUND

In my *Pennsylvania Fireside Tales Volume VII*, a chapter titled "War Whoop and Scalping Knife" contains an account of an Indian raid upon the Patrick Watson homestead in Limestone Township of Union County in 1780. Christian Shively, the Watson's nearest neighbor, was in his field flailing wheat with a flail at the time of the raid and heard the sounds of gunshots coming from the Watson farm.

Shively grabbed his musket and hurried over to the Watson home site, arriving too late to save either Mrs. Watson or her son Patrick. It's believed that that same Shively flail now rests in a museum somewhere in Delaware or Maryland, but there is one other Shively artifact that has an interesting history as well; yet one more artifact of the frontier, if it could be found.

Christian Shively was a pacifist, settling near the mouth of White Spring Run in present-day Limestone Township prior to 1755. Here he was determined to remain, despite any and all Indian troubles. He even went so far as to conceal his wife and two children in his cornfield on one occasion to keep them safe from Indian raiders. Following the Watson massacre, however, Shively decided his pacifist lifestyle would not guarantee his family's safety indefinitely. He concluded that it was time to seek temporary shelter elsewhere and took prompt measures to accomplish that.

Evidently of an optimistic turn of mind, the old homesteader was convinced that the Indian troubles would blow over and he would be able to come back to his homestead at some later date. Therefore, he decided to bury his cast-iron cook stove in boggy ground along White Spring Run, fully expecting to dig it up again when border troubles had subsided and he could return with his family.

He constructed a log raft, lashing it together with hickory withes. Boarding the raft with his family, he pushed it into Penn's Creek and allowed the current to sweep them towards Fort Augusta and safety.

Eventually the frontier wars ended, and Shively eagerly returned to his cabin in the woods. Once there he found that some apple trees he had planted prior to his flight downstream had flourished and were laden with fruit. It was a welcome sight, and, with thoughts of fresh apple pies no doubt dancing in his head, he began looking for his buried cook stove.

He searched diligently but the buried stove eluded him. So much had changed in his absence, so much had been overgrown, that he no longer recognized the spot where he had hidden the precious cooking appliance. He continued his quest for years, and even in his later years he was often seen, stick in hand, prodding the earth at spots where he thought he would find his stove. Then one day, his persistence paid off and his stick struck iron. It was a Eureka moment, and "amid great rejoicing," the old stove was resurrected and restored to its rightful place in his kitchen.[1]

Whether the cook stove eventually rusted away over the years, or it was handed down through succeeding generations of Shivelys as a family heirloom is something that may never be known. Perhaps it sits somewhere in a museum just like Christian Shively's flail, or maybe it resides in a place of honor in the home of one of his descendants.

Regardless of what the case may be, either one is possible, it seems, since even the Shively homestead and barn are still standing and in use yet

---

1. Franklin Ellis and Austin N. Hungerford, *History of the Susquehanna and Juniata Valleys, Volume II*, 1420–1420a.

today in Limestone Township. Both retain their ancient façade, looking much like they must have looked when Christian and his family lived there during the times when the Indian troubles caused him to bury his stove.

HANSEL AND GRETEL

In their colorful and much-loved collection of German folktales, the Brothers Grimm preserved the story of Hansel and Gretel, and how those frightened children dropped breadcrumbs to mark the trail so they could be sure they could find their way back home after being abducted by an evil witch.

A similar tale is preserved in the historical annals of Juniata County, but its authenticity is questionable, because it appeared in a work by an historian whose reputation for accuracy is suspect. However, true or not, the tale may have been a popular one on the frontier back in the day, and so it's included here with the caveat that readers can decide for themselves how much is fact and how much is fancy.

Hansel and Gretel, and other children in the Black Forest of Germany, had to have an almost super-human toughness and tenacity to survive through the Medieval Ages, and the same might be said of the children living on the Pennsylvania frontier during the times of the Indian wars. Many adults were killed and captured during those troubled times, but there were plenty of children who were abducted and slaughtered as well. And one place where this was particularly true was in Juniata County.

War parties often raided settlers' homes in the valleys of the Juniata, and one such incident is said to have occurred between Shaver's Creek and Stone Valley during harvest time in 1782. It was late in the month of October, and no war parties had been seen for months. Indian Summer had come and gone, and since that delightfully mild period of weather was usually the last time Indian raiding parties would venture forth, everyone thought they were safe, that the warriors had returned to their villages in the north for winter.

So confident were the settlers that any savage warriors would not be back until spring that they at first took little notice that Misses Ewing and McCormick had failed to return to Stone Valley from a visit they had made to the Shaver's Creek settlement. Unbeknownst to the frontiersmen the girls had made it to Shaver's Creek, but when returning home along a mountain path, they had been surprised and captured by a war party that had escaped detection.

By the time the girls' parents realized what may have happened, it was agreed that it was too late to try to follow the kidnapped maidens. Neither girl suspected that this was the decision that was made back home, and so they decided to leave a trail with whatever means they had at hand for those who they were sure would soon be in hot pursuit. Both young ladies would eventually be reunited with their families, through prisoner exchanges or by payment of ransom, but their hopes were not to be rewarded this day, despite the clues they tried to leave behind.

When they had been captured, they were carrying some loaves of fresh-baked bread that the settlers at Shaver's Creek had sent back as gifts to their friends at Stone Valley. They clever young ladies decided, perhaps remembering Hansel and Gretel in the Grimms' fairy tale, to break small pieces off the loaves and scatter them on the trail as they went along in hopes that it would give their friends a clue as to their route when they tried to follow. However, their ever-alert captors noticed what the girls were doing, and guessing their strategy, took the bread from them.

The girls then began to break limbs off bushes that they passed along the trail, but their captors once again perceived their object for doing this, forcing them to stop. They traveled for seven days, enduring rain, sleet, and snow, until they reached Lake Erie, where Miss McCormick was given as a present to an old Indian woman who happened to take a fancy to her.

Miss Ewing was taken to Montreal but was released in an exchange of prisoners shortly afterwards. Upon making her way back home she informed Mr. McCormick about his daughter and where he might find her. It was to be a long and arduous journey, but his love for this daughter drove him on until he found her and managed to buy her back from her captors.[2]

AN INDIGNITY ENDURED

General Daniel Brodhead was, in 1780, the commander of Fort Pitt, now the location of present-day Pittsburgh. He needed eyes and ears in the surrounding wilderness so he could be aware of the movements of his British and Indian enemies, and one of his most trusted scouts was Captain

---

2. Uriah J. Jones, *History of the Early Settlement of the Juniata Valley*, 316–18.

Samuel Brady. Consequently, Brady was often sent out of the fort to check for the presence of Indians to the north and west of the fort.

It was a task he relished because he sought revenge. Spurring him on was the seemingly unquenchable hatred he had for the Native American; men who had killed both his father and brother in Clinton County the year before.

And now, during 1780, the war parties had been making raids on pioneer families in both Armstrong and Allegheny Counties, and a raid on the Sewickly Settlement was particularly devastating. Refusing to let this atrocity go by unpunished, General Brodhead ordered Brady to track down the marauders.

Fired with adrenaline, Brady took five soldiers and a friendly Indian and set out to find the raiding party. The detachment eventually managed to find the murdering band and exacted their revenge, but not before Brady had to suffer through a rather unpleasant personal experience.

About six miles north of Kittanning, Armstrong County, Brady and his men found the raiding party's canoes on the banks of the Allegheny River near Big Mahoning Creek. Under cover of darkness the Fort Pitt men crept up to the warriors' campfires. Deciding to get as close as he could, Brady crawled up to a point where he could get a good view but still be concealed by an embankment which provided some cover. After he got himself in position he began to survey his foes.

He noted where they had stacked their muskets, and just as he was counting the number of warriors in the camp, he was alarmed to see one of them throw off his blanket, get to his feet, and begin walking toward him. He knew he could not move without being seen, and so instantly decided to remain where he was and accept the risk, knowing he would have to deal with whatever might happen.

Slowly he lowered his head below the top of the embankment he was using for concealment and tried to remain motionless. But then he felt something like hot tea being poured out of the spout of a teapot onto the hollow of his neck. As the warm liquid trickled down his back and over his chilled flesh, it produced a panicky feeling, he was later to say, that took all his nerve to control.

Like the true frontiersman that he was, Brady's first reaction was that of self-defense. He therefore slowly and quietly reached for his tomahawk, preparing himself to use it when he had it in hand. But he realized that he had discarded it when he had decided to approach the campfires, thinking it may alert the Indians to his presence if it accidentally should drag across stones or gravel.

Girding himself to endure the unpleasant "shower," Brady submitted to this very unpleasant action until it was over. The warrior, having relieved himself and never detecting Brady's presence, returned to his place by the campfire, wrapped himself snugly in his blanket once again, and fell asleep as if nothing was amiss.[3]

NOT A SIGHT TO BEHOLD

During a period of conflict in 1763 known as Pontiac's War, after the Ottawa chief who was the mastermind behind it, raiding warriors attacked settlements as far east as Cumberland County. Their bloody raids threw the entire Pennsylvania frontier into a panic as reports of the uprising spread. Many settlers fled east to Carlisle, still considered a safe haven. But things changed on the third of July 1763, when an express rider from Fort Bedford brought alarming news from the west.

The tired rider immediately rode up to the center of town so his thirsty horse could get a drink from the town watering trough, but news of his arrival spread quickly, and anxious citizens soon surrounded him and showered him with questions. His answers did little to quell their anxiety when he told them that savage warriors had overrun major forts to the west. It was unpleasant news, but his final comment, "The Indians will be here soon!" was the most alarming of all.

The most stalwart citizens immediately mounted their horses and fanned out into the neighboring countryside to warn settlers of the coming doom. To their surprise the messengers soon found roads clogged by panicky frontier families who were fleeing to the reputed safety of Carlisle. Most appeared miserable, bearing countenances of grief and horror, and many reported seeing smoke rising from burning cabins in neighboring valleys. Then there were others who were fleeing from those same burning homesteads and their slaughtered families within.

Upon hearing that the Indians had indeed arrived and had already begun their acts of pillage, a group of armed Carlisle citizens ventured

---

3. Robert W. Smith, *History of Armstrong County, Pennsylvania*, 259–85.

forth to spread further warnings and to bury the dead as they encountered them. History does not recall whether or not these hardened frontiersmen were prepared for the sights they were about to encounter, but at least some of them may have been physically sickened by what they found.

The scenes of carnage that they came upon were vividly described by a notable historian of the colonial period when he noted that when the men reached Sherman's Valley "they found fields laid waste, stacked wheat on fire, and the houses yet in flames, and they grew sick with horror, at seeing a group of hogs tearing and devouring the bodies of the dead. As they advanced up the valley, everything betokened the recent presence of the enemy, while columns of smoke, rising among the surrounding mountains, showed how general was the destruction."[4]

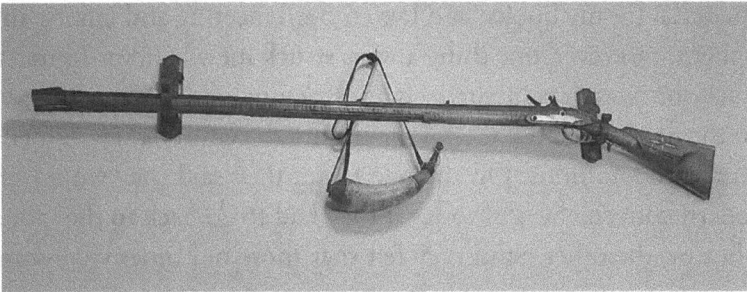

A Pennsylvania Long Rifle and Powder Horn. This replica, with its brass and silver inlays in the stock, was modeled after rifles made by Lancaster County colonial gunsmith Jacob Dickert, who is considered to be one of the most influential gunsmiths during the time of the Revolutionary War. He provided many such rifles for Colonial troops. It is also identical to those carried by Pennsylvania frontiersman during the times when every able-bodied man was a soldier. Musket and powder horn are part of the author's collection.

---

4. Francis Parkman, *The Conspiracy of Pontiac*, 311.

CHAPTER XI

THE TIMES THEY ARE A-CHANGIN'

I've interviewed scores of people over my many years of collecting material for my books, and I've enjoyed meeting and talking to every one of them. However, one thing always struck me whenever I interviewed someone who was "up in their eighties or nineties." When they looked back to the first several decades of the twentieth century, they seemed to do so with mixed emotions. On the one hand, they said they would miss all the modern conveniences of today if they had to go back to the Good Old Days, but on the other hand they felt that those old times were somehow better.

"People didn't have as much as they do today, but they were happier," was the way my grandmother put it. But people back then were not afraid of work. They knew how to work, really work, because they had to do so in order to survive. They didn't have the labor-saving devices or the modern machinery that we take for granted today. Manual labor was the main way the job got done, and the people that did it remembered just how hard it could be.

"I wish the kids today could see some of my days to what they have today!" was the way one octogenarian put it. "They wouldn't believe it! We had good parents, but we worked all right. We'd plant potatoes; we bought cows and we milked; we fed chickens and pigs. We even shocked wheat by hand.

"Dad had a cradle, and he'd cut it and then take so much and binder twine and make little sheaves. He tied them all by hand and when he got so many we'd stick one down and pile so many around and place some on top to keep the rain out. And boy when they came to thresh, would that be a big day for us!"[1]

It may be hard for some today to understand why anyone would look back on such hard times with any fondness. However, the ones who lived through the hard times also remember that there were advantages to living back in those simpler days.

"You know, they lived better than we do today," noted the old gentlemen who was born in 1904 and who had first-hand knowledge of the times of which he spoke. "You know why?" he asked. "They had their own potatoes; they had their own meat; they had their own pork; they had their own lard; and they had their own eggs.

"They had their own wheat to grind into flour and they had their own corn to make cornmeal. All they had to buy was tobacco and sugar and kerosene. And they had their own homemade bread; good homemade butter to put on it. But when they wanted a day off, they took it. They were their own boss!"[2]

And there were times of enjoyment, even though they were much simpler times than would satisfy many today.

"Cherries, that used to be our snack. We'd get hungry for this little snack, you know. So we'd go down and bring 'em up, sweeten 'em, and eat 'em. We got candy, but not like kids do today. We'd make homemade ice cream sometimes. As soon as we got snow, why then we'd take cups and put sugar in and either cocoa or vanilla and milk—fill it up pretty well. And then we'd take spoons and go out and get some clean snow; and boy we'd put snow in, you know, and mix it up until it got thick. It was a good way of growin' up, I guess. I said I guess I'm still the oldest timer around here, and I believe it was the best."[3]

Even the simplest forms of transportation are recalled with delight.

"We didn't go too many places, but Dad, he had a sleigh. He used to put straw in that, and blankets, and that's the way we'd go to town in the winter. Boy oh boy it used to be cold! We'd crawl under the blankets, and we'd wear scarves over our foreheads! If they'd'a dressed like that today, the kids would laugh at ya, wouldn't they?

1. Gladys Brown (born 1905), recorded April 23, 1988.
2. Randall Steiger (born 1904), recorded November 15, 1980.
3. Gladys Brown (born 1905), recorded April 23, 1988.

"We had a surrey too. It was a two-seated thing, and it had like fenders. It was almost like a buggy, but they called it a surrey. It had two seats and a top on it; it had no fringes that I remember. There was like a running board to get in and out. Boy that was a big Sunday morning when we was going to grandparents. Hitch two horses up to the surrey, and away we'd go!"[4]

It seems that all generations in all cultures look back to their own childhood or to their ancestors' times as being better days than those they're living in. There is always the pervasive feeling that something valuable gets lost or discarded in the march of progress. Nor is this sense of loss something that is new to the latter part of the twentieth century. Alexander McClure, in his *Old-Time Notes of Pennsylvania*, published in 1905, felt this same bereavement.

"The memory of the people of those days that comes to me with the sweetest incense is that of the serene content that prevailed among all classes and conditions. No one possessed great wealth, but none were so poor that they could not have food and raiment unless hindered by serious illness.

"In such cases there were always prompt and generous ministrations. The sick and the sorrowing of every community were known in almost every household, and where there was want there was always a most willing supply. No matter how people differed in politics or in religion, or on any of the other questions which at times divided rural communities, the duty of caring for the children of sorrow was accepted by all.

"Religion was the common law, and Sunday was made a day of most tedious and laborious worship. The neighborly feeling that was cherished by all was one of the most beautiful attributes of human nature, and it is a misfortune that it has almost wholly perished as the railroad, the telegraph, the newspaper, and all the other many agencies of progress have transformed our communities of long ago into the unrest of modern and better civilization.

"There can be no great transformation of the tastes and habits of a people without some loss of that which should have been preserved; but, discounted by all the unrest that modern civilization has brought, it has made men and women stronger and nobler, and has vastly greater sources of restraint than were thought of in the quiet of the contented rural life. The house in which I was born and reared, although a brick building and

_____
4. Ibid.

comfortably furnished, never had a lock on door or window, and the burglar, or even the petty sneak thief, was entirely unthought of."[5]

Other "unthought-of" things began to appear as the twentieth century broke upon the scene. One eighty-year-old lady, born in 1894, recalled seeing the canal boats plying their way along the canals of her native Juniata County when she was just a little girl. She also vividly remembered when the first railroad trains began to appear.

According to her, the trains were such a novelty that whenever their schoolteacher heard the lonesome wail of a train whistle, she would dismiss her students so they could run outside and watch the train go by. The first telephones also made an impression upon her, recalling how people thought that they "were really something."[6]

Of course, other amazing innovations were introduced in the early years of the twentieth century, including the airplane, and the automobile or horseless carriage as it was sometimes called. Indeed, by 1916 one in every ten Pennsylvania farmers owned his own car, but the new-fangled vehicles were not always the most reliable means of transportation.

Often experiencing mechanical problems, stranded motorists would sometimes have to listen to the jeers of "Get a horse" from those passing by in their horse-drawn buggies. Nonetheless, it was their first ride in a car that many of these same people would remember for the rest of their lives. Riding along without being pulled by a team of horses was a real novelty.

"I remember the first ride I got in a car," recalled the eighty-three-year-old lady in 1988. "Jim Reeder lived over right from us down here," continued our charming hostess, "and he got this Ford. He told my dad we should get ready because he was coming over to give us girls a ride. Boy oh boy! Boy they had a horn outside, you know, and you squeezed that! He took us down here and up to Harter Lane and fetched us back home. Well, boy oh boy, that was really somethin'; that first ride we got in a car!"[7]

Similarly, when my own ninety-three-year-old grandmother was asked what the most amazing thing was that she had experienced in her lifetime, she immediately responded "the airplane." So, for one lady it was

5. H. H. Hain, *History of Perry County*, Pennsylvania, 503.
6. Mollie Karstetter (born 1894), interviewed July 5, 1976.
7. Gladys Brown (born 1905), recorded April 23, 1988.

the automobile, and for the other it was the airplane, that served as their introduction into the modern era.

Other marvels of the technological revolution included the electric light, with the lightbulb being a major departure from the kerosene lights and candles everyone used for illumination in the past. Some people apparently never did seem to grasp the difference between them at first, and at least one story made the rounds about the man who didn't quite understand what electricity and electric lights were all about.

According to this tale an "old fella" had his house wired for electricity and there was an outlet with a lightbulb in it on the ceiling of his bedroom. When going to bed the first night after it was installed, he went "whoosh" and then "whoosh" again as he tried to blow it out, much like he had always done with his candles.[8]

This preceding story about the man trying to blow out the electric light bulb, just like he always did with his candle, might have circulated as a joke, but it could have just as well been based on an actual event. The fact that, at first, people really didn't understand the electric light is clearly seen in a story from Sunbury, Northumberland County, where in 1883 Thomas Edison constructed the first incandescent electric lighting plant in the world.

On July fourth of that same year his plant began generating current, and people in town were amazed at the plant's lights, which seemed to burn without any flame. One particularly excited person cried out to all those trying to get in for a closer look to "Come and see the funny bottle with a red-hot hairpin in it that makes light!"[9]

Today it seems as though progress is moving along faster than ever before. New technological marvels surface monthly, and the world gets smaller and smaller as all of us seem to be moving toward a greater interdependency. There are certainly advantages to all the technological breakthroughs, but along with them often come unforeseen environmental and societal difficulties.

Nonetheless, the answers to some of mankind's thorniest problems lie in more scientific discoveries rather than in attempts to stifle progress or to

8. Robert Frazier (born 1920), recorded April 23, 1988.
9. Pennsylvania Writers' Project, *Pennsylvania—A Guide to the Keystone State,* 531.

turn back the clock to a simpler day. What is unfortunate, however, is that some things get lost in the advance of progress.

For example, we seem to get softer as luxuries and affluence increase, and at least one old-timer summed that thought up quite nicely when he said to me "I'm afraid if they had to farm today even like they did thirty years back, there'd be a lot less farmin'!"[10]

As time went by and fewer people lived on farms, many city folks developed superiority complexes, having great fun swapping stories that used derogatory names for farm folks, like "rubes," "hayseeds," "clodhoppers," or "hicks." Such jokes about farmers grew in popularity, especially those concerning traveling salesmen and farmers' daughters, and a lot of them were not at all flattering. Most cast the farmer in a bad light.

One such tale arose from the early days of the Depression when the politicians in Washington were trying to come up with ways to put the unemployed back to work. Whether the story had a basis in fact or not is debatable, but supposedly some bureaucrats at that time came up with the idea that they could send teams of city men into the country where they would shoot predators that were bothering farmers' livestock.

"The notion was that the city men would have jobs and the farmers more to sell if foxes, crows, hawks, and the like were exterminated or at least brought under control. One squad of shooters came across a herd of goats and didn't know what they were. They reported to Washington and asked for instructions, describing the goats as strange animals with chin beards, mournful eyes, long dreary faces, and bare behinds. 'For God's sake don't shoot,' Washington responded, 'Those are the farmers!"[11]

And jokes like that would probably have been "fighting words" to some of the more hot-headed husbandmen of the day. Men then were not as ready to fight as they were in earlier days, but fists were still a good way to settle arguments in the 1920s and 1930s. Nonetheless, civilized behavior had come a long way from early pioneer days when fighting was an anything goes exercise.

When frontiersmen had a private quarrel, they would lay aside their rifles and knives before starting to fight, but once they began, they used sticks and fists, with no holds barred. As a result, many such antagonists

---

10. Arthur Auman (born 1909), recorded October 31, 1981.
11. Bud Knoll, "Waddle on the Buffalo Run," *Town and Gown Magazine*, March 1980, 14.

came out of these tussles with ears bitten off or eyes gouged right out of their sockets, and it was the brawniest and strongest men who were most admired.

As might be expected, however, that admiration came with a price. Such men were often sought out by others who wanted to prove that they were stronger and better fighters. It is said that one such contender was a Lancaster County ironmaster named Christian Grubb, who heard about a Moravian brother named Just Johnson.

In 1777, Johnson was landlord of Bethlehem's Sun Inn in Northampton County. The Inn was an establishment known far and wide for its accommodations, but it was just as well known for its landlord and his powerful stature. But Christian Grubb, who was famous for his strength too, and who had some prowess as a boxer, went looking for trouble.

"Just Johnson was an affable Goliath, and it was not until Grubb had grossly insulted him that he finally lost his temper. Suddenly grabbing the ironmaster by the seat of his breeches and the collar of his coat, he hoved him over the iron railing of the porch to the pavement below. 'Gott bless meiner soul,' exclaimed Johnson, 'I drows you over de bannisters!'

"Grubb, who was no lightweight but a man of girth and brawn, was satisfied with Just's display of strength and took it in good part. He told the landlord who he was and why he had come to Bethlehem, and together they made merry over the incident."[12]

A similar story is told about Samuel Hodge of pre-Revolutionary War Adams County. Hodge too was known for his great strength, and another strong fellow from Cumberland County decided he wanted to see who the better man was. One day the Cumberland County chap arrived at Hodge's house and asked Hodge's wife where he might find her husband.

The would-be challenger soon found Mr. Hodge making cider. He told Hodge he had come to fight, whereupon Hodge told the man it was not a good idea. The challenger was persistent, and Hodge finally agreed to accommodate him, with the suggestion that they both first take a drink of cider. Hodge then picked up a huge barrel full of sweet apple squeezings and drank from the bung hole. He handed the barrel to his challenger, who, having seen this display of strength, decided he really didn't want to fight after all, and left with his tail dragging between his legs.

---

12. Edwin V. Mitchell, *It's an Old Pennsylvania Custom*, 152.

A similar account is recorded in the historical annals of Berks County where it is noted that one Dewalt Bieber, born in 1729, "was known as 'Barra Bieber' because he successfully fought with a bear one evening on his farm." Here he's also described as "a very powerful man, being able to lift a barrel of cider to his lips and drink from the bung-hole."[13]

And historical records up in Bradford County preserve the seemingly impossible feats of strength of one William Finch, "a native of Connecticut and a Revolutionary soldier, who was the first settler on what is known as the Towanda Hills. Mr. Finch was a very powerful man. Once a large grey wolf attacked one of his yearlings; he hastened to the spot, seized the wolf by the hind-legs and soon thrashed the life out of him. It is said of Mr. Finch, when 70 years old, that he could take a barrel of cider by the chimes and put it in his cart."[14]

Yet another strong man was once celebrated over in Lycoming County, where Revolutionary War soldier Jacob Tomb Sr., born in 1750, served as a private in Second Company of the Third Battalion, Pennsylvania Militia. While living on the frontier, he treated his Native American neighbors with great respect and thereby garnered their respect and protection.

At least the Tomb property was spared during that perilous time when war parties came down en masse upon frontier settlements. It was a period of such great panic that many settlers fled the area in July of 1778, especially after warriors had burned nearby Fort Antes. But Jacob and his family did not join them. For whatever their reasons for staying, one may have been that they felt they would be spared because of their relationship with their aboriginal friends.

Conversely, the warring natives probably did not care about Tomb's "peaceable, good-natured disposition," but on the other hand they may have been wary of his great physical strength. It was said that he also could lift a full barrel of cider and drink from its bung hole, and that he could also "take two barrels, one under each arm, and walk off with them."[15]

Stories of great feats of strength like those performed by Just Johnson, Samuel Hodge, and others of that same period seem exaggerated, but they no doubt were possible, given the stories that were handed down to us about

13. Morton Montgomery, *Biographies from Historical and Biographical Annals*, 1106. Appears on the Berks County Genealogical website.

14. Clement F. Heverly, *Pioneer and Patriot Families of Bradford County, Pennsylvania*, 324.

15. Spencer L Kraybill, *Pennsylvania's Pine Creek Valley and Pioneer Families*, 1059.

Interior of the Conrad Weiser Homestead cabin. Visitors to the Conrad Weiser Homested historical site in Berks County can tour this well-preserved dwelling which contains many of the items that could once be found in Weiser's, and other settlers', wilderness cabins during the time of the French and Indian War.

the feats of the Conestoga waggoneers during that period of Pennsylvania's history.

According to many first-hand accounts, the waggoneers could "lift a hundred pound keg of nails onto the wagon by grasping the narrow edge of the key between the fingers and thumb of one hand," "unload a six hundred pound barrel of molasses singlehanded," "walk off with a half-ton of pig iron to win a wager, "handle a fifty-six pound weight with the ease of a gymnast throwing a dumbbell," and "lift a wagon off its four wheels by lying under it and pushing upward with both hands and feet."[16]

So just as men and times have passed over the years, things have also changed, as they always do. Looking back over the last two hundred years it's obvious that those changes have been exceptional, and one has to wonder what changes we'll see in the next two hundred. I'm sure those looking back at that time will be amazed at how much things have changed from now until then. One thing seems to be certain, however, and that is that

16. George Korson, *Pennsylvania Songs and Legends*, 239.

there will not be men in the future who are like the Goliaths of Pennsylvania's Colonial past. Indeed, it might be said of them that, like in Genesis 6:4, "There were giants in the earth in those days."

A NOTE ABOUT THOSE CHANGING TIMES:

Times have changed in one important way since the lumbering and mining era in Pennsylvania, when companies had free rein to strip and lay bare the mountains and hills of the state. I was reminded of that one day in 2018 when driving north on Route 44 from Woolrich in Clinton County to Waterville in Lycoming County. Suddenly I was slowed to a stop by a red light. Signs indicated that there was road work ahead, and soon it was obvious that the southbound lane of the highway was totally closed off.

It did not take long to see that a long section of that southbound lane had broken away and fallen into the ravine below, leaving nothing but a gaping canyon where an asphalt highway had once passed over it. It had been that way for two months, we later learned, because road crews had no idea of how to repair things.

As I sat there pondering over the situation, the thought crossed my mind that "nature has a way of showing us who's boss," and that's as true today as it was in Joseph Trimble Rothrock's time. As Pennsylvania's first State Forester, he, and other determined conservationists like him, had foresight enough back then to protect the natural beauty around us. They did so by creating the State Forests, State Parks, and Natural Areas we now enjoy, and which are thus preserved for future generations. I therefore pray that those in power today and in the future will be as foresighted and as respectful of those same resources as time goes on.

Joseph Trimble Rothrock saved Pennsylvania's state forests and was instrumental in creating the many state parks we enjoy today. Although not of Rothrock's stature, I like to think of myself as his compatriot. Pennsylvania's verdant forests would have been lost forever without his intervention. Likewise with the Pennsylvania legends and folktales that I have preserved on the printed page. They would have been lost forever as well, without my determination to save them for posterity.

CHAPTER XII

PIG'S EAR? YELLOW DOG?
TORPEDO? GUM STUMP?

In *volume VI* of the *Pennsylvania Fireside Tales* series there is a chapter titled "What's in a Name?" In that chapter I mentioned that I was always intrigued by the many unusual place-names that appeared on the road maps and topographical layouts of the state. I also stated that I was not only fascinated with the names, but was also curious as to how those names were chosen as a designation for a mountain, creek, town, or valley. I proceeded to offer possible explanations as to why the unusual place-names had arisen.

It was also fun in that chapter to group the names together, as possible desirable places to live for those whose current places of residence may not be appealing to them, or places to live that may be more appropriate given their occupations or avocations. As examples I mentioned that those who live in Drab (Blair County) might prefer Beautiful (Franklin County), and magicians would probably be most happy living in Presto (Allegheny County) or in Eureka (Montgomery County).

There were many other delightful comparisons as well, but that chapter, I later realized, was not all-inclusive. Since then, I've found other fascinating Pennsylvania place-names that intrigued me as well, and they appear in the pages that follow. However, just like for some of the place-names in *Volume VI*, in some of the cases that follow the place-names are just that; the towns that once stood there are now just ghost towns, the companies around which they flourished having shut down and moved away.

Nonetheless, the names serve as a historical record; a last reminder of the people and the industries that once thrived there. They provide some amusement when their history is revealed, but they can also tweak our imaginations or evoke curiosity when the story behind their names cannot be discovered.

At least for the following place-names I hope that the reader's curiosity will be somewhat satisfied. Even though the explanations offered may seem implausible or vague, they are probably the best that can be discovered at this late date. Therefore, I once again have to leave it up to the reader to decide just how much is fact and just how much is fancy—similar to the same cautionary approach I've recommended to my readers when it comes to many of the legendary tales found in this and other chapters in the Pennsylvania Fireside Tales series.

ALTHOM STATION (WARREN COUNTY):

Once a major railroad shipping point for the area's lumber and silica sand industries, railroad officials came up with the name for the small settlement that grew up around it using the AL part of the nearby Allegheny River and THOM part from the last name of Robert Thompson, a local man who was a river pilot and owner of large tracts of land in the area.[1]

BABYLON (WARREN COUNTY):

Reputedly once the hometown of a man named Ben Hogan, who lived here during the oil boom years of 1866–68, and who was derided as "the wickedest man in the world" by his neighbors. He received that title because he maintained a house of ill repute in the town. Local lore states that the town name came from the day when a traveling minister rode by Hogan's establishment and was shocked to see naked ladies cavorting in the yard. He stopped long enough to comment to the townspeople that "This is the wickedest place I have ever seen! I name it Babylon!"[2]

BENDIGO (ELK COUNTY):

Named for English bare-knuckle boxer William Bendigo, whose name is an apparent corruption of Abednego, one of the trio of Shadrach, Meshach,

---

1. Ernest C. Miller, "Place Names in Warren County, Pennsylvania," appeared in the January 1971 issue of *the Western Pennsylvania Historical Magazine*, 15–36.
2. Ibid.

*A Valley's Namesake. Born in 1861, Perry J. Krise was
the first to settle in the small valley that bears his name in
the Centre County foothills of the Seven Mountains. The
picture, taken in 1937 when the valley was still a veritable
wilderness, is unique, since photos of a man who was the
original settler in a valley, thus affording him the honor of
having it named after him, are rare. (Photo of Perry Krise
courtesy of Mr. and Mrs. Paul Wilson.)*

and Abednego—three men whose story in the Old Testament tells of how
they emerged unscathed from King Nebuchadnezzar's fiery furnace. Boxer
William Bendigo became bare-knuckle champion of all England in 1835
and was inducted into the Boxing Hall of Fame in 1955. That he had fans
in this part of Pennsylvania is evident from the fact that they decided to
name their town after him.[3]

---

3. Unknown author, "Elk County Name Derivatives," Fall 1997 issue of *The Elk Horn*, Elk County
Historical Society.

BOOT JACK (ELK COUNTY):

The layout of the town boundaries reminded people of the shape of a boot jack, a sling-shot shaped device with its V-shaped notch used for pulling off boots, and so the name seemed appropriate to those who were tasked with coming up with an acceptable name for the little settlement.[4]

BROAD AXE (MONTGOMERY COUNTY):

Named after the Broad Axe Tavern which, after opening in 1681, became the favorite gathering place for the community that grew up around it. Here the local news was read to the citizenry on a daily basis, and many travelers found it to be an ideal stopping place where they could always find good food and a warm comfortable bed. Somehow, unlike many other wayside taverns of the period, the Broad Axe managed to stay open throughout the Revolutionary War, and local lore even states that General George Washington often led his troops past the Broad Axe.

Since it was such a community favorite, it did not take the citizenry long, when trying to decide upon a name for their town, to agree that it should be named after the tavern, which took its name from a colorful sign hanging over its main entrance. Upon the sign there was a depiction of a square, a compass, and a large broadaxe. The tavern was in continuous operation until closing in 2019. Until then it had the distinction of being the oldest bar in Pennsylvania, and perhaps even in the entire United States.[5]

BROKENSTRAW (WARREN COUNTY):

A place originally named by aborigines as Cushanadauga or the "place of broken grass." When they explored this same region, in 1739 and 1749, the French, upon seeing the vegetation here, called it the place of "cut straw." Eventually the community that grew up here utilized parts of both names when choosing a name for their settlement.[6]

Ethnobiologists have concluded that there may have been several varieties of tall grasses that provided the basis for the name, all of which could grow to a height of up to six feet. When dying off in the winter, the plants

---

4. Ibid.

5. Edwin V. Mitchell, *It's An Old Pennsylvania Custom*, 53; information from "Only in Your State" website, January 18, 2018.

6. Ernest C. Miller, "Place Names in Warren County, Pennsylvania," appeared in the January 1971 issue of *the Western Pennsylvania Historical Magazine*, 15–36.

would fall over, and the dead stems would cover the ground with a thick layer of "broken straws."[7]

BURNT SHANTY RUN (CENTRE COUNTY):

Although no explanation as to the source of this name could be found, the following account from Elk County is suggestive. In 1818, when Dr. A. M. Clarke was eleven years old, his father moved his family from New York State to the "wilderness of Pennsylvania." It took six weeks traveling via a wagon pulled by oxen, and the eleven-year-old sometimes had to drive the team. It would have been quite an adventure for a lad that young, and the sights and sounds of the wilderness were indelibly imprinted in his mind, especially along a rough road they found near present-day Luthersburg.

Later he would write that they took "the Fox, Norris & Co. Road over the mountain, which was really just a path, and followed our journey over the hills and mountains. Finding we could not get through in a day, we had to stop overnight at a place where the road-makers of Fox, Norris & Co. had built a shanty which had been burned, so it was called the 'burnt shanty.' Here our wagon-cover gave us a good shelter, and a good spring of water to drink from was pleasant indeed."[8]

CASTLE GARDEN (CAMERON COUNTY):

In order to accommodate the steady influx of immigrants into this country during the last half of the nineteenth century, it was decided that there needed to be an official place to process the mass of people disembarking from the ships in New York Harbor. Consequently, in a collaboration between the city of New York and the government of New York State, the "Castle," America's first immigration center, was created at the tip of Manhattan Island.

It soon became known as "Castle Garden," but today, as one of the major landmarks within the 23-acre Battery Waterfront Park, it is known as Castle Clinton National Monument. A large contingent of immigrants that came into this country through the Castle Garden Immigration Center settled just outside what became the borough of Driftwood.

---

7. Charles E. Williams, "What was the 'broken straw' of Pennsylvania's Brokenstraw Creek? An investigative ethnobotany of place," *Proceedings of the Society of Ethnobiology*, May 5, 2011.

8. William J. McKnight, *Pioneer Outline History of Northwestern Pennsylvania*, 494–512.

When that borough was created it was decided that, for better tax revenues, it should include the railroad shops in the area but not include the immigrants in the adjoining area, which then became known as Castle Garden to reflect the place where the majority of the residents had come into this country. The little community still bears that name today.[9]

CORYDON (Warren County):

There is some doubt as to the origins of this name, but there is a township of the same name in McKean County. No evidence has been found as to the origin of the McKean County name either, but it has been conjectured that the name may have its basis in the poems of Greek poets where it appears as the name of a shepherd in both Theocritus's *Idylls* and Virgil's *Eclogues*.[10]

DAGUS MINES (Elk County):

The name of this small village was derived from two sources. The post office was opened here in 1880 when the Northwestern Mining and Exchange Company started its extensive mining operations in the area. Local residents wanted to refer to those mines when choosing a name for the town since they were such a prominent feature of the topography. They also decided to use the first part of the name of Daguscahonda, a nearby hamlet whose Indian name means "place of pure water."[11]

FOOT OF TEN (Blair County):

So-named because it was located at the foot of the tenth inclined plane of the Allegheny Portage Railroad. Famous for being the first railroad that linked the Midwest and the Eastern Seaboard, the obstacles to build it across the seemingly insurmountable barrier of the Allegheny Front and its steeply inclined gaps were formidable. Nonetheless, the civil engineers of the time were up to the task, and part of their solution was the utilization of steep cable-railway inclined planes that used steam powered windlasses

9. Information provided by Cameron County Historical Society; and also found via online searches.

10. Ernest C. Miller, "Place Names in Warren County, Pennsylvania," appeared in the January 1971 issue of *the Western Pennsylvania Historical Magazine*, 15–36.

11. "Tells How Places In Elk County Received Names," *Ridgeway Record*, Ridgeway, Pennsylvania, July 16, 1932. Courtesy of the Elk County Historical Society.

to pull the trains up the inclines, much like the mechanisms used on modern-day ski lifts.[12]

FORCE (ELK COUNTY):

When the coalfields opened up around here in 1900, the town was built to accommodate the coalminers and their families. Originally named Byrne in honor of Major John Byrne, president of the coal company that opened the mines, the name was changed to Force in honor of one John Force, who was a local character whose actions and personality endeared him to local residents.[13]

FORTUNETELLER CREEK (FULTON COUNTY):

No information can be found regarding this name origin, but its basis may be the same as that noted under Nancy's Creek in Bucks County (see below).

GUM STUMP (CENTRE COUNTY):

Once a stop on the Snow Shoe Branch of the Pennsylvania Railroad, it is now merely a place name. Here there is very little in the way of houses or other structures, and the stump for which it was named, if that is the case, is no longer in evidence either. That stump may never have existed at all. Instead, the name for the place possibly arose from some local wag who borrowed it from the stages of comic opera where the name was often used when referring to small and insignificant towns.[14]

HERMIT SPRING (WARREN COUNTY):

This town was named after a hermit named Samuel Wallace, who for many years made this ever-flowing spring his home. Angered by the way he was being treated by his parents, the strange recluse left his home in the Erie County/Crawford County region during the 1860s and settled here. He raised a cow, and had a fine vegetable garden, but also depended on berries he found in the forest for his food supply. He was a hunter, tanning the

---

12. National Park website: www.nps.gov/alpo/learn/historyculture/index.htm.
13. "Tells How Places In Elk County Received Names," *Ridgway Record*, Ridgway, Pennsylvania, July 16, 1932. Courtesy of the Elk County Historical Society.
14. Paul M. Dubbs, "Where to Go and Place-Names of Centre County," compilation of articles appearing the in the *Centre Daily Times*, State College, Pennsylvania, 1959–60, 36.

hides of deer he had shot and then sewing them together for clothing. He disappeared to parts unknown when oil from a renegade oil well polluted his spring and made the water unpotable.[15]

HUSBAND (SOMERSET COUNTY):
Named after one of the most notable pioneer citizens in that area, Harmon Husband, a farmer who was best known as a radical author and preacher. His many self-published pamphlets espoused liberal political reforms of all kinds. His extreme behavior lead to his arrest and incarceration on numerous occasions.[16]

LAMENTATION RUN (FOREST COUNTY):
Ebenezer Kingsley was one of the first pioneers to settle along Tionesta Creek, and as one of the first to explore the area, he assigned names to most of the streams he found near his homestead. Many of these names were based on a personal experience he had at that stream. In the case of Lamentation Run in Forest County, for example, he assigned that name to the creek because he once "heard doleful cries of animals near its mouth."[17]

LEATHER CORNER POST (LEHIGH COUNTY):
Named from a pre-Revolutionary War inn called the Leather Corner Post. That name, so it is believed, came from a large wooden post standing outside the inn to which someone once nailed a very expensive cut of leather. The leather was not there long until it was stolen, but its subsequent reappearance sometime later created a mystery that never was solved but which indelibly imprinted that name upon the spot where the post once stood.[18]

NANCY'S CREEK (BUCKS COUNTY):
An old woman here was known for her powers as a fortuneteller, and her reputation gradually spread throughout the region, causing her business to thrive. Her little log cabin along the creek was located about a half mile up

15. Ernest C. Miller, "Place Names in Warren County, Pennsylvania," appeared in the January 1971 issue of the *Western Pennsylvania Historical Magazine*, 15–36.

16. Mary Elinor Lazenby, *Herman Husband: A Story of His Life*, 1724–1795, 125–80.

17. Michael A. Leeson, *History of the Counties of McKean, Elk, and Forest, Pennsylvania*, 835.

18. Mike O'Hara, *Origins of Town Names of Northeast Pennsylvania, no page # given*.

from the creek's mouth, and locals often referred to the stream as Nancy's Creek since that was her first name.[19]

OWL'S NEST (ELK COUNTY):

Named from the first family to settle here, the Ohls' family name was pronounced just like that of the nighttime feathered hunters whose weird cries often penetrated the dark woods surrounding their little cabin "nest" in the mountains.[20]

PEANUT (WESTMORELAND COUNTY):

This place is not named after the lowly goober pea grown in Georgia; nor is it based on peanut butter, the peanut's delicious derivative. Pea coal and nut coal are sizes of anthracite coal, with pea being one of the smallest and nut being slightly larger. Both types were produced in mines in this area. The residents of the small mining town that grew up here, when having to choose a name for their village, decided that a combination of both these coal sizes would be an ideal title. The idea that they named it after peanut butter probably originated in November of 1996 when town residents created a forty-foot-long peanut butter and jelly sandwich, thought to be the world's largest, for the Peanut Advisory Board's celebration of peanut butter.[21]

PIG'S EAR (ELK COUNTY):

The forests through here were alive with "woods hicks" during the boom days of the lumbering era, and many of the workers were unmarried virile young men who longed for female companionship and charms. Not surprisingly, these potential customers attracted at least one whorehouse establishment to open up for business nearby. The Pig's Ear thrived for a while, but its business declined as the lumber and its customers gradually dwindled away, and then it too disappeared, leaving only its name behind to remind us of the delights that this pleasure palace once provided.[22]

---

19. http://bethlehemtownship.org/history.html.

20. Unknown author, "Elk County Name Derivatives," Fall 1997 issue of *The Elk Horn*, Elk County Historical Society.

21. US Geological Survey Geographic Names Information System: Peanut, Pennsylvania; Peanut Advisory Board "Peanut, Pennsylvania Celebrates Its Namesake," 1994.

22. Unknown author, "Elk County Name Derivatives," Fall 1997 issue of *The Elk Horn*, Elk County Historical Society.

PUDDINTOWN (CENTRE COUNTY):

So-named, it was believed, from a delicacy enjoyed by all the members of one of the first families to settle here. The treat in question was what they called "white pudding," and it was made by mixing boiled lard, seasonings, and white flour. They reserved holidays and Sundays as the days on which they would eat their special homemade "pudding."[23]

RASSELAS (ELK COUNTY):

One of the most prominent men in the public affairs of this part of the county was a man named Rasselas Wilcox Brown. He was respected by his contemporaries, and so they honored him by assigning his first name to the community that grew up here.[24]

RED HOT (ALLEGHENY COUNTY):

Today the exact location of this place-name is hard to find. No historical accounts seem to pinpoint its whereabouts, and when I visited the area in 2019, I could find no local residents who had ever heard of the place. One lady who grew up in the township (West Deer) claimed that as a child she had heard that Red Hot was the name of a local coal mine, which seems plausible since this entire region today is still actively strip mined.

No local histories have references to any such mine, but it may not be unreasonable, on the other hand, to speculate whether or not the origin of this name might have arisen in the same way as that of Pig's Ear in Elk County (see above)!

In asking other locals in nearby communities whether they had heard of Red Hot and suggesting that the name may have come from a house of ill repute, one man said that it was a reasonable assumption. He noted that during the hey-day of the coal-mining and lumbering industries in that section there were many towns that had one or more bordellos, including the nearby town of Mayport which during its industrial boom had at least three such recreational spots.

ROUGH AND READY (SCHUYLKILL COUNTY):

Located in Upper Mahantongo Township of Schuylkill County, it is mostly a place-name today with only two houses and a church. Its name was based

---

23. Paul M. Dubbs, "Where to Go and Place-Names of Centre County," compilation of articles appearing the in the *Centre Daily Times*, State College, Pennsylvania, 1959–60, 53.
24. Ibid.

on a hero of the Mexican War who led his Texans into battle in 1845. His soldiers gave Zachary Taylor the nickname of "Old Rough and Ready," and his reputation as a war hero helped him win election to the office of President of the United States in 1848.

SKY TOP (CENTRE COUNTY):

Sky Top is the name for a spot and a small village along Route 322 that crosses the ridge tops of Bald Eagle Mountain near State College. The pull-off here offers a panoramic view of many mountain ranges cascading away in the distance and an overlook of the town of Julian in the Bald Eagle Valley below. The breathtaking views no doubt inspired original settlers here to choose the name of Sky Top for this place since it must have seemed to them like it was at the very top of the sky.

STARBRICK (WARREN COUNTY):

Starbrick was named for the Star Brick Company, which, during its early years of operation, made clay bricks with an imprint on them of a large star. At first the bricks sold almost as fast as the company could make them, due to a building surge in Warren, but then, around 1908, the company closed its operations due to the fact it had exhausted the clay supplies on its land.

However, it's said the boys in Warren still sought out the star-imprinted bricks for their own purposes. They had found that if they melted lead and poured it into the recessed star image on the bricks, they could make a decent copy of a sheriff's badge![25]

TALLEY CAVEY (ALLEGHENY COUNTY):

There is a Talley Cavey Road in Allegheny County, but it does not lead to a town of that name today. Instead, it takes the traveler past the town of Allison Park, which, it turns out, was called Talley Cavey back in the 1700s. Early Irish settlers here named their town after Tullycavy on the Ards Peninsula outside Greyabbey, County Down, Ireland. The name comes from the Gaelic term meaning "hill over the borough."[26]

---

25. Ernest C. Miller, "Place Names in Warren County, Pennsylvania," appeared in the January 1971 issue of *the Western Pennsylvania Historical Magazine*, 15–36.

26. Information found online.

TORPEDO (WARREN COUNTY):

This town was named in remembrance of a frightening episode that occurred near here in 1882. Although it is called "fracking" today, one of the tried-and-true techniques used by oil companies to increase production in their oil wells back in the earliest days of the industry was called "shooting the well."

The process involved packing an iron cylinder about the size of a large thermos with fifteen to twenty pounds of nitroglycerine or black powder. A blasting cap was stuck on the cylinder, which, when thus charged, was referred to as a "torpedo."

The torpedo was lowered into a well and then detonated by dropping a heavy weight down upon it. The process was not without its risks, and people were reminded of that one day in February of 1882 when a wagonload of glycerin meant for charging oil well torpedoes was struck by a train. The event was reported in the *Titusville* (PA) *Herald* under date of February 24, 1882, and read as follows:

"If accidents are ever fortunate, such a one occurred last Wednesday (February 22) night. Fred Cohensquire was on his way to Clarendon with a load of 880 pounds of glycerin, driving the splendid grey team which once did service on the Brunswick carriage. While crossing the Dunkirk, Allegheny Valley & Pittsburgh railroad at Ross' switch, one of the animals caught his foot between the rail and a plank and fell down. The driver, knowing it to be about train time, made efforts to release the fallen horse but could not succeed. He had removed the other horse when the rumble of the train was heard, and summoning a Swede nearby he began unloading the wagon of its dangerous load.

"Probably not over one-half of the load had been removed when the train, the express due here at 7:40 in the evening, dashed around the curve. Engineer Daniel Beam immediately reversed the locomotive and applied the air brakes, but the short distance and the speed of the train prevented a full stop. The engine struck the horse, cutting both legs and also tilting the wagon about halfway over but very luckily the glycerin did not explode. The chances are that had the wagon gone clear over, the explosion would have occurred and undoubtedly caused a great destruction of life and property. The horse was shot by one of the passengers and put it out of misery. The train men and passengers of course were startled by the sudden stoppage but hardly realized what a narrow escape they had had. The more they discussed the matter the more they became frightened, and when their train reached this city they were a pretty excited lot. Conductor Nelson had charge of the train."[27]

WHISTLETOWN (ELK COUNTY):

Reportedly named after the habit of a town celebrity named James W. Gallagher, whose constant whistling provided a source of entertainment and fond memories for those who lived there with him.[28]

WHITE HALL (MIFFLIN COUNTY):

This small settlement in the Kishacoquillas Valley of Mifflin County was no more than a small cluster of homes. It no longer exists as such today, but the Whitehall General Store, along Route 655 midway between Belleville and Allensville, preserves its memory. The town's name reportedly has facetious origins, supposedly based upon the wide hallway of the local tavern. That passageway was initially painted white, and when repainting was needed, the white color was always retained.[29]

YELLOW DOG (ARMSTRONG COUNTY):

Mining companies exploited their workers in many shameful ways during the coal mining era of the 19th and early 20th centuries in Pennsylvania. The low pay, unsafe working conditions, and long hours led to the formation of the United Mine Workers Union and subsequent improvements in the mineworker's lot.

One thing the mining companies did provide for their workers was good housing, realizing that proper living conditions and a sense of community boosted morale. Such was the case for the town called Yellow Dog, near present-day Worthington. The town was settled in the late 1800s when abundant iron and limestone deposits were found in the region.

The deposits were a long distance from the nearby towns where workers lived, and so they pleaded with their employer, The Pittsburgh Limestone

---

27. Ernest C. Miller, "Place Names in Warren County, Pennsylvania," appeared in the January 1971 issue of *the Western Pennsylvania Historical Magazine*, 15–36.

28. Unknown author, "Elk County Name Derivatives," Fall 1997 issue of *The Elk Horn*, Elk County Historical Society.

29. Lewistown Old Home Week Committee, *Historical Souvenir of Lewistown, Pennsylvania*, 19.

Company, to provide housing closer to the work sites. The company agreed to do so, providing their employees would agree that they would never unionize.

The workers acceded to the company's demands but thereafter their town became known as "yellow dog" to remind others that they were cowards (or "yellow dogs") for agreeing to the no-strike contract they had signed with their employer.

The mining communities flourished as long as the industries that spawned them stayed in business, but when the depression of 1893 hit, it led to a decline in the mining industry, and many of the mining communities became ghost towns. The village of Yellow Dog managed to thrive for many decades, even up until recent years.

Then the closure of the mine, pollution of the town's well water, and the collapse of the housing market in the early 2000s, finally sealed its doom. Today only a handful of homes can still be found there, and the town has passed through the hands of several owners, but the present ones plan to turn the place into a historic site where visitors can learn about its history and also take classes in sustainable living.[30]

---

30. "Only in Your State" website, April 28, 2016, www.onlyinyourstate.com/pennsylvania/yellow-dog-pa/.

CHAPTER XIII

HELL HATH NO FURY

When historians wrote their accounts of Pennsylvania's Indian wars, they rarely mentioned the part played in those troubles by the colonial women of that period. Some might say that those omissions were due to male chauvinism, males of that period giving little respect or credit to the women of their day. Although chauvinism was no doubt a factor that could have been behind the oversights, it appears that there may not have been that many noteworthy instances where frontier women were directly involved in fighting savage warriors in the first place. Nonetheless, there are a few accounts in the colonial record that are noteworthy, and which reveal how strong and tough women on the Pennsylvania frontier had to be, and could be, when a situation demanded it.

One such episode from the southeast corner of Greene County, near the West Virginia border, is a perfect example of that female heroism. It was one instance where a colonial woman in that section refused to be intimidated by marauding warriors. Her name was Experience Bozarth, and her heroic actions inspired one historian of that county to preserve her story to show how she "acquitted herself in defense of her own life and that of her husband and children."[1]

Just as the old adage that states that "Hell hath no fury like a woman scorned," it might just as well be said that "Hell hath no fury like a mother defending her children," and the story of Experience Bozarth provides convincing evidence that supports the truth of that saying.

---

1. Samuel P. Bates, *History of Greene County, Pennsylvania*, 550–51.

Old engraving of illustration of Indian Attack on Outlying Plantation (artist unknown).

It was a cold day in March 1779, when a visitor to the Bozarth cabin along Dunkard Creek in present day Greene County would have found three neighboring frontier families huddled in fear in the Bozarth homestead. Afraid to stay alone in their own cabins and deciding that they were safer when together, the families had congregated there when learning that local rangers had reported seeing a marauding war party on the top of nearby Bald Hill.

That afternoon the families' children, who had been playing outside, came running into the cabin in a state of heightened agitation, exclaiming that they had seen "ugly red-men."[2] One of the men in the Bozarth cabin immediately stepped into the open doorway of the cabin to check out the children's report when a loud musket report echoed through the surrounding forest and the man fell back into the cabin dead, a musket ball embedded in his chest.

Almost immediately the brave who had fired the shot rushed into the cabin; its momentarily-stunned occupants could only look on as he attacked the sole other man within. The tough frontiersman was more than

_____

2. Ibid.

Seneca leader Guyasuta (c. 1725-1794). Late 18th century painting, artist unknown.

a match for his savage attacker, however, managing to throw him onto a bed, and calling for a knife to kill him.

The only occupant who had recovered her senses enough to come to his aid was Mrs. Bozarth. Not being able to find a knife at hand, she picked up a nearby axe and with one swift adrenalin-infused blow de-brained the Indian. At the same instant a second savage appeared in the doorway, causing Mrs. Bozarth to turn and take several swings with her axe at him. Her blows proved to be as effective on the second attacker as they had been on the first, as one of them slit his stomach open, causing his entrails to appear.

Upon seeing his wound, the severely wounded attacker, bawling out in pain, turned and fled outside. His companions, busy at killing the children who had been unable to flee to the cabin for safety, heard his cries and came running to help him.

When one of them stuck his head inside the cabin, it was Mrs. Bozarth's quick thinking that saved the day once again. Taking her axe and swinging it once more, she cleaved in the head of the hapless attacker, knocking him flat onto the ground. A third attacker managed to drag his wounded

Statue of Chief Guyasuta
(1720–1794), located at
Main Street, Sharpsburg,
Pennsylvania (photo taken by
the author in April 2019).

Inscription on Guyasuta's Statue.
It reads as follows: Guyasuta ("Crosses
Standing in a Row), a leader of the
Seneca Tribe whose hunting ground
included the Sharpsburg area, served
as George Washington's guide during
a 1753 survey of the point. He later
represented his people in negotiations
with the British settlers. During his
later years, he settled in the area
now known as Guyasuta Reservation
and was probably buried in the area
now occupied by the north end of the
Highland Park Bridge.

GUYASUTA (1720 - 1794)

Guyasuta ("Crosses Standing in a Row), a leader of the
Seneca Tribe whose hunting ground included the Sharpsburg
area, served as George Washington's guide during a 1753
survey of the point. He later represented his people in
negotiations with the British settlers. During his later years,
he settled in the area now known as Guyasuta Reservation
and was probably buried in the area now occupied by the
north end of the Highland Park Bridge.

comrade away, whereupon Mrs. Bozarth, and the man who had been shot and now somewhat recovered, pulled the cabin door shut. Here the brave little band in their log fortress, along with the corpses of the dead neighbor and the dead savage, held the other warriors at bay for three days until help finally arrived.[3]

Almost three years later, in the summertime months of 1782, there was yet another lady on the Pennsylvania frontier whose actions once again supported the claim that "Hell hath no fury like a mother protecting her children." It was during July of that summer that a hundred Seneca warriors under Guyasuta, their great war chief, invaded present day Westmoreland County and laid waste to Hanna's Town (now spelled Hannastown), then the county seat of that county.

Emboldened by their success, the warriors, flushed with victory, attacked other nearby communities with deadly affect. Some paid the ultimate price for their boldness, but most got away without a scratch, except for one unfortunate warrior who had the misfortune to challenge a singularly brave young lady.

On that particular day, along Turtle Creek and near present-day Murraysville in Old Westmoreland, Susanna Rea was in the family homestead alone, preparing the noon meal for her brothers who were at work in the fields. A stealthy warrior, who had been observing the place from afar and who was waiting for a chance to collect another scalp, stealthily advanced to a window in the side of the cabin. Although he took extra care to avoid any noise, he must have inadvertently stepped on a twig or stick that caused the young woman in the cabin to turn and see him starting to crawl in through the window.

He had just placed his hands on the windowsill, and so it gave the brave and quick-thinking maiden time enough to seize a nearby axe that was propped up on the side of the kitchen table. Bringing it down hard on one of the man's hands, her blow "severed it at the wrist," and the surprised warrior turned and ran, his screams of pain echoing through the forest.[4]

According to the historical records, there were about 60 men, women, and children huddled inside the Hanna's Town stockade on July 13 when the main Seneca attack under Chief Guyasuta occurred. The stockade was

---

3. Ibid.
4. C. Hale Sipe, *The Indian Wars of Pennsylvania*, 670–71.

Replica of the fort at Hanna's Town, located at Hanna's Town Historical Site in Westmoreland County A 2019 view of what remains of the old Forbes Road from the time of the French and Indian War can be seen through the open gate of the fort. On the other side of the road is a reproduction of Robert Hanna's cabin which contains many interesting artifacts of the period. It was on this spot on the Forbes Road that Peggy Shaw rescued the small baby that she saw sitting there.

large enough to afford them all some protection, but only about twenty men had muskets to provide firepower for a defense. Expecting to take them by surprise, the Senecas crept up to the stockade in silence, and then, shooting and yelling out their war cries, they rushed in among the settlers' log houses.

The defenders inside the cabins took turns at the musket loopholes cut in the logs. All being good marksmen, they kept their assailants at bay until nightfall. Then, under the cover of darkness, the Senecas managed to set fire to the cabins. Luckily for those inside the fort, a strong north wind kept the flames from consuming the stockade. By morning reinforcements from other nearby settlements began to arrive, and the marauders thought it wise to depart with many captured horses heavily laden with stolen household goods.

Only one resident of Hanna's Town was killed during that attack, and to this day the poignant story of the "Heroine of Hanna's Town," as she

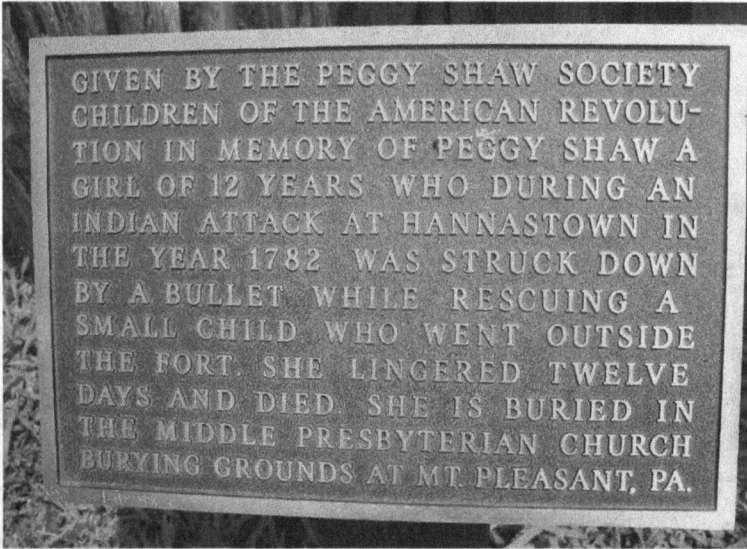

Peggy Shaw Memorial at Hanna's Town Historical Site in Westmoreland County.

is often referred to, is repeated at local historical societies in hushed and respectful tones.

Margaret Shaw, or Peggy as she was called by the Shaw family and their friends, came from sturdy pioneer stock. Both her brothers, David and Alexander, were hunters and frontier scouts, serving as rangers to help protect settlements from Indian attacks. Their many engagements with war parties established their reputations as frontier fighters and as staunch defenders of the border.

David had returned from his service in the Continental Army just five years earlier and had dedicated himself to the defense of the settlements where his family lived. And when the attack on Hanna's Town occurred, David's first action before seeking protection for himself inside the fort was to make sure his father's family had reached there in safety. It's therefore not surprising that his sister Peggy displayed similar courage and a similar concern for others that same afternoon.

Throughout that morning the able-bodied defenders within the fortress, men and women alike, were busy fretting over the best ways to ward off an attack on the fort. But their focus on self-defense meant that their attention to the safety of their children became lax. And so it happened that during the course of the afternoon a small child wandered out as far as the fort's picketing and within range of the attackers' musket fire. Seeing the danger the child was in, Peggy Shaw ran over to it, intending to carry it back to safety. But just as she bent down to pick up the toddler, she was struck in the chest with a musket ball, which entered her right lung. Her death was not instantaneous, and she suffered greatly for two weeks. Unable to eat or drink during that time, she was nothing more than skin and bones when death finally claimed her. Her mortal remains were buried in the graveyard of the Presbyterian Church two miles north of Mt. Pleasant.[5]

NOTES:

1. Although the residents of Hanna's Town were urged to rebuild their homes, few did. Five years later, the Westmoreland County seat was moved to nearby New Town (modern-day Greensburg, PA). The area of the Hanna's Town settlement became agricultural land, preserving the remains of the town under the surface of tilled fields.[6]

2. The site of Hanna's Town was excavated, beginning in 1969, and yielded more than a million artifacts of the daily life of the early inhabitants. Today the Historic Hanna's Town site is located just off U.S. Route #119, midway between Greensburg and New Alexandria, PA. The site includes the reconstructed Robert Hanna Tavern/Courthouse/homestead, three vintage late-18th century log houses, a reconstruction of the Revolutionary-era fort and blockhouse, and a wagon shed housing an authentic late 18th century Conestoga wagon.[7]

---

5. J. N. Boucher, *History of Westmoreland County, Pennsylvania, Volume I*, 171–85.
6. Ibid.
7. Ibid.

CHAPTER XIV

DELIVERANCE

In the previous chapter we described a number of incidents where pioneer women accorded themselves with amazing displays of courage and physical prowess when fighting off Indian attackers on the Pennsylvania frontier. However, not all such encounters ended with favorable outcomes for the women who had the misfortune to come face to face with marauding warriors.

Many of these "tough-as-nails" females ended up as captives and were marched off to distant Native American villages to either be tortured or to become assimilated into the aborigine lifestyle, never to see friends or family again. Some of their stories can be found in previous volumes of the *Pennsylvania Fireside Tales* series. Therein are a number of accounts describing many unfortunate episodes just like this. On the other hand, if we turn to both the historical record and to oral history, we can find more stories that tell of women who seem to have made some miraculous escapes from savage war parties who wished to do them harm.

Among the more interesting and numerous tales of this type are several from Westmoreland County that have come down to us from the descendants of the defenders of that great Westmoreland County frontier fort called Fort Ligonier. Built by the British army in 1758, this sturdy stockade, in its eight years of existence, never was overrun by an enemy force.

Decommissioned in 1766 after the end of the French and Indian War, the abandoned garrison gradually deteriorated until it disappeared from the landscape. Remnants of the place remained, however, and when archeologists and historians decided to build a replica of the old fortress starting in 1949, they were able to discover outlines of the architectural layout and even recover remains of the fort's powder magazine.

Visitors to the replicated structure today will see what is described on the Fort Ligonier website as the "finest recreated 18th-century artillery collection in North America." They can also take a guided tour of the fort and visit the fort's museum, where many artifacts from the battles that occurred there are on display.

During Fort Ligonier Days, held annually from October 11–13, guests are entertained by firing of the fort's cannons. However, these physical reminders of the fort's illustrious history do little to remind us of its colorful human history, tales of human interest that tell of events that once occurred there, but which have faded away almost as completely as the fort itself once did. Nonetheless, for those willing to seek them out, those types of stories can still be heard from the families that have preserved them for their descendants.

View of reconstructed Fort Ligonier (taken in 2018) with "Friesian Horses" in the foreground. The "horses" were wooden obstacles with sharpened fraises, sometimes shod with iron, and were used to block entrances or to close gaps in the fort's walls.

Views of two of Fort Ligonier's 18th century artillery canons.

View of Fort Ligonier armory.

Once such family is the Ulery family, whose ancestors once lived within two miles of Fort Ligonier during the time of the French and Indian War. Like all pioneer families in the area at that time, the Ulerys would seek refuge in the fort when there were warnings of an impending Indian attack. Even then, however, there were still crops to tend to and to harvest. That was the case one hot July afternoon when there had been no warnings of imminent savage incursions. The Ulery's crops needed tended to, and so the three Ulery sisters, Abigail, Elizabeth, and Juliann, were sent out to work in one of the fields.

In the midst of their back-breaking toil the three young women, focusing on the chores they needed to complete, did not notice a stealthy band of warriors creeping through the woods next to the field. Then, to their great consternation, the girls were surprised to see the savages almost upon them, whereupon the frightened women immediately broke and ran toward their home.

The two oldest sisters, Elizabeth, age 18, and Juliann about 20, soon outdistanced Abigail, age 16, who tried her best to keep up, but she soon fell far behind. Thinking their younger sister had been overtaken and captured, Elizabeth and Juliann, upon reaching the house, ran inside and barred the door.

When she did reach her homestead young Abigail found she could not open the door. Unable to speak because of the panic that had seized her, she was unable to tell her family it was her; and those inside, seemingly thinking that she was one of the savage warriors that was pounding on the door, would not let her in. Seeing that her assailants were almost upon her, the forsaken lass sped away into the woods behind the cabin.

The pursuing marauders at that point ignored her and rushed to the cabin door, which they, in unison, tried to push open. Mr. Ulery, realizing what was happening, grabbed his musket and fired it through the sturdy oak planks of the door.

There was a howl of pain from the other side, and the assailants gave up. Unable to break down the door and probably fearing another shot, the frustrated raiders departed. Along with them they carried off their moaning companion who had been wounded in the bowels. They headed in the direction that they had seen young Abigail take.

The resourceful young lady had only run a short distance when, seeing a hole in the ground left by a large tree that had been uprooted in a storm, she decided to use it as a hiding place. The decision had been prompted by the fact that the hole was thickly overgrown with weeds and was littered with many fallen leaves, all of which enabled her to adequately conceal herself. Here she laid as still as possible for several minutes before she finally heard her pursuers come up to her place of concealment and begin searching for her.

They realized it made a good hiding place, and thinking the leafy branches of the fallen tree would be where they would find her, they made a thorough search through them, ignoring the roots. Once they determined she was not in the branches, one of them said they should keep looking. He said he was certain she was there somewhere because he "could smell her," and that they should scalp and kill her once they did find her. At this point the petrified woman thought her end had come, until deliverance came from an unexpected source.

The wounded warrior had been moaning piteously the entire time his comrades had been searching for their quarry. Taking pity on him, his

The Ulery door. The bullet hole is just below the middle cross piece on the right side of the door. The planks used by Mr Ulery to construct the door are not as thick as one might expect. (Photo taken by the author at Fort Pitt Museum in Pittsburgh, July 2019. My thanks to Mike Burke of the museum staff who gave me a tour or the museum and graciously arranged for me to take the photos shown in this book.)

fellow warriors decided to abandon their search. With that, one got on each side to support him; and they carried him away, disappearing over the brow of a nearby hill.

Once she realized her pursuers had gone, Abigail jumped up and ran back to her family, where she was greeted with great joy. Years later, when telling her grandchildren and other fascinated listeners of her narrow escape, she would say that she still looked back upon it as one of her life's greatest trials.

This was because, she noted, it had taken every ounce of her willpower to keep from jumping up and running away while the savages were searching for her. She also would say that her fear at the time was compounded by the concern that her rapidly-beating heart would cause movement in the leaves that were covering her, thereby revealing her to the Indians.

Some months after their thrilling escape, the Ulerys found a freshly-dug grave on the other side of the hill over which the warriors had fled

Another view of the Ulery door (photo taken by the author at Fort Pitt Museum in Pittsburgh, July 2019).

with their wounded companion. The internment convinced them that the man had certainly died from his wounds.

The Ulerys also preserved the oaken door from their cabin, after moving into a more commodious dwelling. They claimed that it always reminded them of how lucky they were to be alive. It is said that the door, with the telltale bullet hole, is still in the hands of their descendants.[1]

As unusual as the preceding tale may seem, there is a similar story of yet another Fort Ligonier pioneer family whose daughter experienced an unexpected form of deliverance from sure death at the hands of bloodthirsty warriors, and her story has also been handed down through generations of her descendants.

During 1763, the year that saw the end of the French and Indian War, it became customary for friendly bands of Indians to visit Fort Ligonier when they passed it on their travels. The commandant of the fort, Lieutenant Archibald Blane, always instructed his men to treat them with respect and to show them around. And so it was that one day in 1763, when a group of them was visiting the fort, James Means, with his wife and eleven-year-old daughter Mary, arrived there as well.

---

1. Ibid, 94–96.

The young pre-teen was quite lovely for her age, and she was so beguiling to one of the visiting Indians that he managed to strike up a conversation with her. He told her that his English name was Maidenfoot, and she informed him that she lived just a mile from the fort.

They conversed for some time, and when the two finally parted, the young man took a beautiful string of beads from around his neck and placed them around Miss Means' neck. Later, when she and her parents were discussing the Indian and his gift, they all agreed that he had seemed heartbroken and dejected when he was talking to her; that the beads must have held some very special meaning for him and were probably one of his most prized possessions. They also became one of Miss Means' prized possessions as well, since they were so rare and so beautiful, and so she often wore them around her neck.

The following spring there came warnings of warriors being seen in the neighborhood again. So, taking no chances, Mrs. Means and her daughter, who was wearing her necklace at the time, decided to head toward Fort Ligonier and the safety it would provide. As they neared the fort, the women were taken by surprise by two large Indians who dragged them into the woods. There they bound the women to two large saplings using deer thongs they had brought along with them. They warned their captives to remain silent or they would be tomahawked.

The bound and helpless women listened for hours as sounds of musket fire and war whoops came from the direction of the fort, making them realize that the fortress was under attack by a hostile force. Later that afternoon all became still, and a lone Indian appeared before the prisoners. The women, thinking that he was there to take their scalps, also felt that their end must be near.

However, when he bent down over them, the lone warrior did not use his knife to scalp them but instead cut the thongs that bound them fast to the saplings. It was then that the women saw that the man was Maidenfoot. They also realized at that moment that he had recognized them at once because of the necklace around the young woman's neck.

The young warrior escorted the women back to their homestead where they met Mr. Means. Here Maidenfoot told them that to save their lives, they must hide in a ravine he pointed out to them to the south. Here he said they must remain until the war party left, which would be in a short while. Then, before walking away, Maidenfoot took a handkerchief from the girl; a white kerchief with her name in black silk lettering.

Having no other options, the Means family decided to follow Maidenfoot's instructions. It was good advice, as they were neither discovered nor harmed by any marauding warriors that day. It was an unexpected deliverance from the least-likely source, and they never forgot it as the years passed by.

As time went on, Mr. Means moved his family out to lands in the west and purchased a large farm near where Cincinnati stands today. There the parents died, and their daughter Mary met and married an officer of the Revolutionary War named Kearney.

He and his wife Mary farmed the land her parents had farmed until he was called back to duty under U.S. Army general Anthony Wayne. Captain Kearney fought with Wayne at the Battle of Fallen Timbers in 1794, a battle that proved to be a decisive victory over the Northwest Indian Confederation, thus securing white settlement of that former Indian territory known to Americans as the Ohio Country.

After the fight at Fallen Timbers had ended, Kearney and the men in his company were walking over the battlefield when they noticed an aged Indian sitting on a log and waving a white handkerchief over his head. Kearney's men wanted to shoot the man on the spot, but Kearney stopped them and, walking over to him, began talking to him.

The old man told him his fighting days were over; that he had fought at Ligonier, Bushy Run, Hannastown, at Wabash against St. Clair, and here at Fallen Timber, and now he only wanted to live in peace.

When they examined the handkerchief the man was using as his truce flag, the soldiers saw it had been embroidered with the name of Kearney's wife, "Mary Means." Kearney, having often heard from his wife the story of Maidenfoot's beads, and how they proved to be her means of deliverance when she was a child, inquired as to the Indian's name. Upon discovering it was Maidenfoot, Kearney took him to the Kearney homestead.

Mary Means and Maidenfoot immediately recognized one another, despite the passage of thirty-one years, and they shared their memories of that melancholy day near Fort Ligonier when their paths had crossed a second time. Mary Means told her old friend that she had always treasured the beads he had given her because they had once saved her life.

He in turn told her that he had always kept her handkerchief, because when he gave her the beads, he had adopted her as his sister, without having any desire to take her from her real parents. He did so, he said, because a short time before meeting her and her parents in Fort Ligonier he had lost his own sister, who was about the same age and size as Mary was at that time.

Captain Kearney and Mary took Maidenfoot in as part of their family and he proved to be an affable and adaptable companion, staying with them for four years until he died of consumption. He was buried with full military honors in a small churchyard outside Cincinnati. To this day the marble slab marking his grave is still there with an inscription that reads "In memory of Maidenfoot, an Indian Chief of the Eighteenth Century who died a civilian and a Christian."[2]

Fort Ligonier's history, and our recounting of women's amazing deliverances from sure death at the hands of savage warriors, would not be complete without mention of the race won by one young woman when she was fleeing for her life.

This interesting anecdote was preserved as part of the Shannon family's oral history, being handed down from one generation to the next and on down to the present day. Like our previous accounts this one also took place during the trying years of Pennsylvania's Indian troubles; in particular in 1778.

During the perilous summertime of 1778 families were still permanently "forted" at Fort Ligonier, but the virile young men and women therein kept themselves entertained by competing in various athletic games, including foot racing. Men and women alike would race from one side of the fort to the other in an attempt to win the crown as fleetest of foot, but the two fastest runners turned out to be a man named Shannon and a young lady named Miss Reed.

The two would often challenge one another, since either one could easily outdistance any of the other runners in the fort, and more than once, either through her natural ability or because of Shannon's chivalry, Miss Reed came out the winner. Whatever the case may have been, however,

---

2. Ibid, 108–10.

Miss Reed's innate athleticism proved to be her means of deliverance when she needed it most.

During the particularly hot and muggy days of July 1778, there were daily reports of savage depredations throughout the Ligonier Valley. Nonetheless, ignoring these stark reports and knowing that they could face certain death, men could be seen leaving the safety of Fort Ligonier every day because they needed to tend to their crops or face starvation in the coming winter.

In order to conduct the work they needed to do in safety, the men left in parties of five or more, with the idea that some of the men would do the work and the others would be posted as guards along the edges of the fields. Then one particularly appealing afternoon, a party of two young men and their sisters could no longer endure being "cooped up" inside the walls of the fort and so decided to venture out to a nearby clearing to pick elderberries.

The clearing was about two miles from the fort, and it was reported that the berries were so plentiful this year that they were weighing down the branches of the many bushes that grew there in profusion. Visions of the berries must have been dancing in the heads of the young people as they walked down the path to the berry patch, particularly since the path was cleared most of the way. However, at one point the roadway passed through a thick patch of underbrush, which at some points formed an arch over their heads.

The darkness there caused them some alarm, but they were somewhat relieved when they saw Major McDowell returning to the fort on horseback. He had been out guarding the farmers in the fields, but his posture on his horse and the way he was nonchalantly carrying his rifle on his shoulder gave no appearance of any concerns. Then suddenly shots rang out from rifles carried by a party of warriors hiding in the thick undergrowth that lined the roadway.

The two young men were in front of their sisters, and one of the warrior's musket balls killed George Reed immediately. Another ball struck the stock of Major McDowell's rifle, causing it to split and send splinters flying into McDowell's face and neck. Young Means had turned and started running back to the girls, who had started running away as well, but the warriors soon surrounded him and made him a captive. His sister was holding onto Miss Reed's arm as they fled away, but one of their pursuers soon caught up with them and grabbed Miss Means, who let go of Miss Reed.

A tearful reunion. The display depicts the following remarkable and touching event: "In 1764, an expedition under Col. Henry Bouquet departed Fort Pitt to reclaim all of the captives taken by Indians during the French and Indian War. Among the many returned were Eleanor Kincade and her son, Andrew, with whom she was pregnant at the time of her capture. Her husband, William, was among the volunteer soldiers on the expedition." History does not record the fate of the reunited couple. (Photo taken by the author at Fort Pitt Museum in Pittsburgh July 2019.)

Freed from her impediment, Miss Reed took off like a scared rabbit, and the fastest Indian, suspecting an easy capture, sped off after her. The race was an even one for the first hundred yards, but the man, seeing he was losing ground, let forth a series of hideous screams and yells, hoping to confuse and intimidate his prey.

His ploy had the opposite effect, causing Miss Reed to feel an extra burst of adrenaline, which in turn allowed her to put an even greater distance between herself and her pursuer. The warrior, however, perhaps trusting that his powers of endurance were far superior to that of this young upstart woman, kept in pursuit.

He maintained his chase until within half a mile of the fort, when he saw the figure of a young frontiersman carrying a rifle. Intimidated by the gun, he veered off into the underbrush and retreated.

The screams of the Indian and the sounds of gunfire had alerted the fort that the young people were in trouble. Young Shannon, fearing the worst for the young woman for whom he had developed a deep affection, immediately recruited a rescue party, which hastened off toward the sounds. The winded Miss Reed, upon seeing her young admirer, threw herself into his arms and collapsed with exhaustion.

The two returned to the fort while the remainder of the rescue party went on to determine the fate of the others. Eventually they found the lifeless bodies of young George Reed and that of Miss Means lying where they had fallen. They also realized that Miss Means' brother had been taken away as a captive.

Miss Reed and Shannon were married some years later after the end of the border troubles, and they settled down on a farm in the Ligonier Valley, living happily there until both had almost reached the proverbial "four score and ten" milestone. However, before dying they would most certainly have learned about the fate of the Indian who had doggedly chased Miss Reed that summer day in 1763. Their source of the information was Mr. Means, who somehow had managed to return from his captivity in 1766.

According to Mr. Means, the Indian who ran after Miss Reed was the most athletic specimen in his tribe; he was so highly respected for this prowess that he had been picked as the future husband of the chief's daughter. After returning to his tribe, however, he was unmercifully derided for losing a race to "a white squaw" and his status had fallen considerably. Mr. Means said that at that point the chief's daughter treated him with nothing but "scorn and contempt," and his fellow tribesman did the same, treating him like a drudge by heaping upon him the crudest and lowliest tasks that no one else wanted to perform.[3]

---

3. Ibid, 110–12.

CHAPTER XV

THE LAST ELK?

With the exception of the moose, there were no larger "big-game" animals in Pennsylvania at one time than the Eastern elk. Larger even than their western cousins, they were impressive by any standards. A fully-grown bull elk could weigh up to 1,200 pounds, stand up to five feet or more at the shoulder, and sport a set of antlers spanning six feet in length. Little wonder then that a bull elk was at the top of a serious hunter's wish list, stirring him to spare no effort in trying to track down and shoot these once-in-a-lifetime trophies.

Moreover, farmers shot them too, because a herd of elk could ruin a field of crops if they found the plantings to be particularly appetizing. So though great herds of elk once roamed across the entire state, the unrelenting slaughter that began in the 1700s eventually began to take its toll, with evidence of the elk's decline beginning in the eastern part of Pennsylvania in the late 1700s.[1]

By 1800, the Eastern elk was exterminated in the Blue Mountains, and forty-five years later it had vanished from the Poconos as well. The decline accelerated with the advent of the lumber industry; and as men cut, slashed, and burned their native habitat all over the state, the elk herds continued to shrink, until by 1890 they were gone. They were then declared officially extinct and listed with the state's other extinct species, that included the panther, the wolf, the Carolina parakeet, and the passenger pigeon. It was a declaration that led some to reflect about how plentiful the elk had once

---

1. Explorepahistory.com/hmarker.php?markerId=1-A-13F

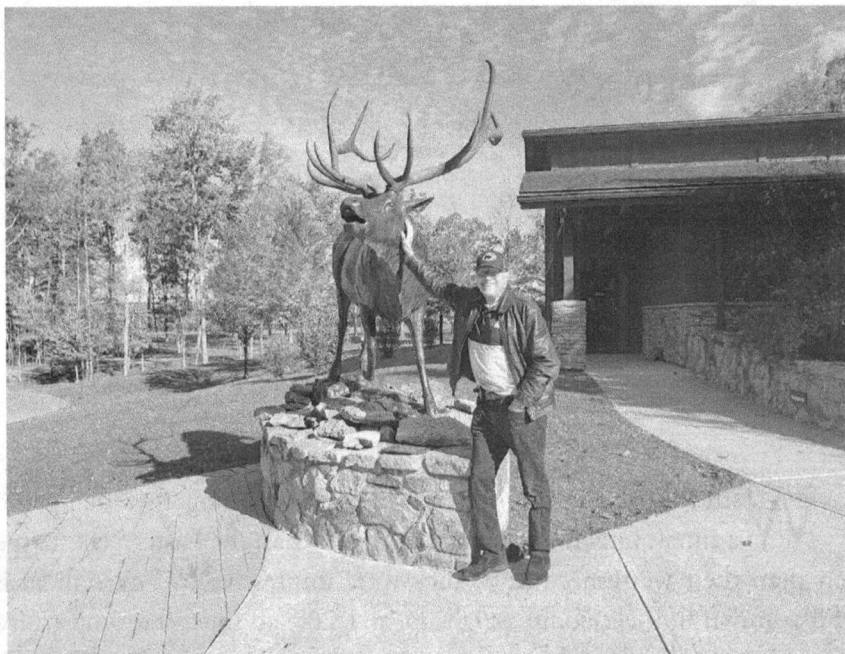

The author standing beside a large steel statue of a bull elk outside the Elk County Visitor Center, Elk County, Pennyslvania.

been. Others wondered who had the right to claim to be the slayer of the last native elk in the state.

"When I started, in 1826, to amuse and profit myself in this section by following the chase in Northern Pennsylvania," stated Colonel Noah Parker, of Gardeau, McKean County, for an article published in the Pittsburgh Post dated April 19, 1896, "elks were running in those woods in herds. I have killed elks on the Sinnemahoning and Pine Creek waters and down on the Clarion River and West Branch that were as big as horses."[2]

The Northern Tier counties of McKean, Potter, Elk, Tioga, and Cameron were the areas where the elk seemed to flourish the most and to last the longest. Some of the earliest elk hunting experiences in that section were preserved by early Potter County settler Edgar O. Austin who, writing on March 4, 1901, stated "I settled at my present residence, now in the borough of Austin, in 1856, then a perfect wilderness. On the First Fork of the Sinnemahoning near Prouty Run was the 'Great Elk Lick' of this

2. Samuel N. Rhoads, *Mammals of Pennsylvania and New Jersey*, 33–34.

region. About 1835 or '36 the first settlers came into this region. The elks with other wild creatures then reigned here in their glory."[3]

Austin also became friends with some of those who had "settled within three or four miles of this lick," noting that "Clifford Hoskins, Charles Wykoff, the Jordans, and John Glasspy, with others, were among the prominent hunters of the time," and that, as a young man, he could not get enough of the stories about what they had seen.

"They all told me," noted Austin, "that they would go to the elk-lick to get a deer as often as they wanted one in the summer-time. Here sometimes fifty or more could be seen at a time, with the fawns playing around like young lambs. Cliff Hoskins said he went there once to get a deer, when he saw several elks in the lick and more in the clearing around it.

"It being the first time he had seen elk there he gazed in wonder, when more came in until forty or fifty had congregated. He watched their grim play for some time and then shot one. The rest started back, then stamped around their fallen comrade, gazing in a bewildered way before stampeding away with the noise of thunder as Hoskins approached."[4]

Austin also recalled that his aunt Eleanor Wyckoff lived within two miles of the elk lick and that she was initially skeptical of tales her brother would tell her about the number of elk he would see there. Finally deciding to call his bluff one day, she had her husband take her there, when other men reported that the elks had come back in force. Describing what she saw to Austin, she recounted "First some came, then more, until the clearing seemed full of them and the men said there were about fifty there."

Describing the lick and the habits of the elk in greater detail, Austin wrote "Regarding the clearing above mentioned—where the elks frequented a big lick they rubbed their horns against the trees, sometimes in play or to rub off the velvet or skin from the new horns. This process soon kills the trees, except the big old ones, so that a clearing of two, three, or four acres is made around the lick. A few thorn trees come up on it which grow so low and stout as to defy them, when it is called a 'Thorn Bottom.' Elks are gregarious, living in small herds if unmolested, likely in families, but they congregate at the licks in summer in considerable herds."[5]

3. Ibid.
4. Ibid.
5. Ibid.

As noted earlier, the elk were much-sought-after hunting trophies, but not just because of their magnificent antlers which dwarf those of a deer and grow up to six feet long, with six or seven tines on each. The elk were also a good source of meat since they grew to be as large as a horse or larger; but for a time they also were a good source of income if captured alive, which was not an uncommon practice if prices were right. Hunting elk to capture them alive, however, was not an easy endeavor, and one such hunt is described by an early settler in the wilds of northern Pennsylvania around 1822. Philip Tome's account provides a vivid pen picture of how stark and dangerous the unbroken wilderness of those days could be, and how intimidating it was to someone who was not used to its challenges.

"John Campbell and myself hired another man named Avery, and went out about twenty miles for an elk hunt," begins the account that the rugged mountain man penned for future generations. "Having established our camp, Campbell and myself left the next day, leaving Avery to keep camp. For three days we hunted without any success, and returned to the camp. During our absence Avery had been kept in a state of alarm by wild animals. Two panthers and eight wolves had prowled around the camp, and so terrified him that he declared he would not stay alone in the woods for all the elk in them!

"We wanted him to remain until we had taken an elk, which he agreed to do, if he could be with us while we hunted. We accordingly took him with us the next day, but when we returned to our camp at night, he was nearly exhausted, having waded through deep snow all day, and the following day was quite willing to remain in camp."[6]

Tome goes on to describe how he and Campbell left Avery to guard their camp again. This time they sneaked out so as not to have to take him with them. They subsequently searched for three full days before finding the tracks of a large elk. They let their dogs loose, following the elk's trail through two and a half feet of snow before finally cornering him on a large rock. Here they managed to lasso it and kept guard over it that night.

"The next morning we started for the camp. Arriving there about eleven o'clock we found Avery with a sad tale," recalled the old hunter, who always enjoyed including this humorous aside when telling the story of his last roundup of a live elk. "Avery said that after our departure the wolves kept

6. Philip Tome, *Pioneer Life; or, Thirty Years a Hunter*, 105–8.

howling around the camp as night began to approach, and his examination into the stores revealed the cruel trick we had played upon him.

"When the suspicion flashed upon his mind that he was doomed to pass another night here, with no company, save that of the wolves and panthers, which might possibly form a repast of him before morning, he gave vent to his feelings in a flood of tears. The next day he resolved to leave camp, and go home, but before he had proceeded more than a mile, he heard the howling of wolves, and as he had no gun, hastened back to the camp."

Tome goes on to relate how the distraught Avery, upon realizing his comrades had gone off without telling him they would be gone for at least one night, if not more, resolved to hunker down and dig in. "He had a good knife, an axe, and a tomahawk, and to these means of defense he added clubs and pointed sticks," noted Tome. "He also kept a large fire constantly blazing, and built a scaffolding about five feet high, on which he slept. He passed the time, notwithstanding all these precautions, in constant anxiety, and was heartily glad to see human faces again, but when he learned we had captured an elk, he was much more delighted."

The men went back to where their lassoed elk had been tied to a tree, only to find it had chewed through the rope and fled. They managed to track it down and capture it again and lead it back to their camp. From there they followed Kinzua Creek into Cattaraugus County, New York, where they were able to make some money showing off their catch. From there they went on to Ellicottville, where they sold their elk for one-hundred-ten dollars. "This was the last elk I ever caught," wrote the sturdy mountaineer, "the low price obtained for him making the business so unprofitable that I abandoned it entirely!"[7]

Tome also noted, in his further ruminations about elk hunting, that younger ones could be easily domesticated and would do the same work as a young horse or steer. He further claimed that the early settlers around Kane, McKean County, were able to domesticate an elk to the extent that they could hitch it to a yoke and have it pull a plow while plowing their fields.

So impressed was Tome with the possibilities offered by domestication of elk that he expressed the opinion that they should be a farmer's standard

---

7. Ibid, 122–23.

livestock, rather than cattle, much like a Laplander's reindeer.[8] This claim
was supported by Col. Noah Parker, pioneer settler of McKean County. In
a letter published on April 19, 1896, in the *Pittsburgh Post*, he writes that
Pine Creek settler Ezra Pritchard, "secured a pair of elks, broke them, and
for a long time drove them in farm work like a yoke of oxen!"[9]

Indians, on the other hand, were not as sanguine about elk hunting,
often bemoaning the fact that they had wantonly turned over to the white
settlers virtually the entire West Branch Valley on the north side of the
Susquehanna between Lycoming and Pine Creeks. Their chagrin was well-
founded because the region had been one of their best hunting grounds,
"always filled with deer and elk, on account of the fine grazing, and hunting parties invading it never came away empty."[10]

It is somewhat ironic, however, that Native Americans were among
the slayers of the last elk in the state. However, there were a number of
men who could claim that distinction, depending upon which section of
the state was being considered. Nonetheless, it is generally agreed that one
claimant as the last slayer of a bull elk in Pennsylvania could be John D.
Decker of Centre County. Decker, it is believed, killed a large bull that his
wife saw in a clearing behind their log cabin, one afternoon in 1877, when
the elderly couple was busy "schnitzing" apples for making apple butter.

Decker grabbed his musket and felled the bull elk with one shot, hanging its antlers on his woodshed, where they remained for many years until
they fell down and were devoured by porcupines.[11] The old woodshed was
still standing when I was a young lad, frequenting the valley with my father
during hunting season, but it is no longer there. However, the original
Decker log cabin still stands today in the valley that bears Decker's name, a
stark reminder of that stalwart pioneer and of the wolves, deer, and elk that
once made this same valley their home.

It is also believed that the last elk slain in Tioga County was shot in the
Algerine Swamp around 1860. This section is now preserved as a Pennsylvania Natural Area in Tiadaghton State Forest, and the story of the killing
of the last elk here has been preserved through folktales handed down in
that same region.

8. Clayton Auman (born 1885), recorded October 31, 1981.
9. Samuel N. Rhoads, *Mammals of Pennsylvania and New Jersey*, 33–34.
10. John F. Meginness, *Otzinachson*, 322.
11. Clayton Auman (born 1885), recorded October 31, 1981.

Not the last elk, but the last stop for this one! Taken inside the Elk County Visitor Center, this bull elk is a taxidermist's pride and joy. This was the only bull elk we saw that day, or any elk at all for that matter. The elk were in peoples' front yards and in almost any open field when we visited there several years ago, but on this October day in 2019 there wasn't a single live elk to be found anywhere! It seems they move in and out, and today they were out!

"There was an Indian named Gustavia Bennett who lived out there in the Algerines. He was considered a 'half-white' since his father married an Indian from up on the Barrens back of Cedar Run, and they had family on the Algerines. He came up Pine Creek with Lyman and lived around Slate Run in later years. I heard the story of the last elks here from Gus Bennett, Gustavia's grandson," recalled the old farmer who had grown up in the Northern Tier.

"The Algerines at that time was almost impossible to get to, but the north-south trail went through the middle of the swamp. But you gotta remember that at that time the Algerines was fairly barren—all this country was—because of the "big burn"; a massive forest fire that swept through here at one time. It was burnt off the same as the Big Trostle and most of the country over there—Bear Run and over in that had no timber on, just brush.

"But that's where the elk was; come up over here from the Big Trostle and over into Lebo and that area. And old man Gustavia Bennett would hunt them elk down and shoot them and take the teeth out and sell them in Philadelphia for high-priced money for just for teeth for the Elk Lodges. It was probably one of Gustavia Bennett's elks that was the last one shot in Tioga County."[12]

There is yet another Native American whose claim to be the slayer of one of the last elk in the entire state may be hard to dispute. Particularly since the killing was verified by the local hunters from whom he stole the prize along the deep waters of the Clarion River in Elk County in 1867. Moreover, one of those local hunters professed to his dying day that the tale of that last elk was his favorite hunting story. This was surprising to his fellow hunters, since in his lifetime of hunting and trapping, he had killed scores of deer and bear, and, as the last of the mighty hunters of that period, helped bring about the extinction of wolves, mountain lions and the mighty elk too.

Ira Parmenter was around ninety at the time of his death in 1899, but his real age may have been a few years less or a few years more since he wasn't sure of his exact birth date. His father, who came from Connecticut in the late 1700s, was one of the first settlers at the "forks" of the Sinnemahoning, near present-day Driftwood, Cameron County, and he taught his son the ways of the forest.

The young man grew up when the virgin forests all over Pennsylvania were still teeming with elk, wolves, and mountain lions, which he referred to as "panthers," the popular name at that time for this formidable beast. He excelled in the skills of the chase, following the life of a hunter and trapper until at age eighty-seven he became partially blind and had to hang his rifle up on the wooden pegs over his stone fireplace one last time.

From that day forward Parmenter had to content himself with telling the tales of his hunting days, and for many years he made the claim that he was the slayer of the last panther in the state. He held on to that belief for decades until an old Pike County hunter named Jacob Bensley brought forth conclusive proof that he, and not Parmenter, was entitled to be awarded with that palm. But Parmenter's claim that he was in on the

---

12. Howard Heggenstaller (born 1921), recorded November 16, 1989.

hunt that ended the life of the last elk shot in the state was one that he could make without anyone contradicting him.

For many years it was thought that Seth Nelson, of Round Island Station in Clinton County, had shot the last Pennsylvania elk in Elk County in 1845. As evidence of that claim, the head and antlers of Nelson's massive Elk County Wapiti made their way to the Peale Museum in Philadelphia where they were on display for years and touted to be those of the last elk shot in Pennsylvania.[13]

Some years later, however, one day during the fall of 1867, Parmenter and his friend Seth Nelson, the same slayer of the 1845 "last elk," were hunting at the head of Bennett's Branch near Driftwood, Cameron County, when they sighted a deer trail and began to follow it. Just as they were getting closer to their quarry, however, they heard a distinctive whistle that seemed to pierce the thick mantle of the dark forest through which they were trying to find their way. Being seasoned hunters they realized that this distinctive sound came from a bull elk, which only made that call at that time of year; the mating season when the bull was looking for a mate.

The deer they were trailing was soon forgotten. The men had brought their best tracking hounds with them, and the dogs soon picked up the elk's smell. The two hunters followed the elk all day, but then the hounds lost it when a heavy downpour washed away the scent.

The nimrods had no choice but to abandon their search that day, but for weeks afterwards they attempted to discover the elk's whereabouts, making daily treks through the wilderness without success. It had not taken anywhere near that long for the word to spread throughout the region, and even as far north as the Indian reservations in New York State, that a lone bull elk was still alive along the Sinnemahoning.

The news seemed to reignite the fire for the hunt that had almost been extinguished in the heart of one old New York State Seneca living on the Cattaraugus Reservation. He had achieved a degree of fame for his hunting prowess over his lifetime, and so Jim Jacobs vowed he would join in the chase once again.

Several months later, in late November of 1867, Parmenter and Nelson woke up to find that a good tracking snow had fallen during the previous

13. Pennsylvania Game Commission website, "History of Elk in Pennsylvania"; Ira Parmenter's obituary, *New York Sun*, (no date given); Pennsylvania Genealogy Trails website, "Genealogy Trails Potter County Pennsylvania Obituaries and Death Notices."

night, and they immediately agreed that it provided a good opportunity to try to find the lone elk of the Sinnemahoning once again. They searched for days, finally finding its tracks in the light skiff of snow along the Clarion River, and this time they were able to follow it through an unforgiving and unbroken wilderness for several more days before being slowed by a blinding snowstorm.

They knew that the elk would not travel in the storm, and so they kept on until they found its tracks leading into a laurel thicket at a place called the Flag Swamp. This marshland was located near present-day St. Mary's in Elk County, but it is no longer there, since it was drained when the railroad was graded through the region.[14] Realizing that their quarry was now within their grasp, the men started to close in on the elk but stopped in their tracks when the crack of a rifle shot rent the silence of the wintry forest.

The surprised hunters followed the sound of the report into the center of the laurel thicket and there, in a large thorn bottom clearing, they found Jim Jacobs triumphantly standing with one foot on the dead elk, calmly holding his rifle in his hands. The wily hunter had used his knowledge of the elk's habits and instincts, cultivated during his past fifty years of hunting the animals, to track it to its hiding place.

Although disappointed that it hadn't been one of them who shot it, Nelson and Parmenter agreed that the old Indian's hunting skills and knowledge had bested them. Therefore, in an act of respect, they helped Jacobs skin the beast and then aided him in carrying his prize to his home in Salamanca. It was said that Jacobs displayed the head and antlers of that same elk on a wall in his house until the day he died, and for all anyone knows they may be hanging there yet.[15]

Nelson would later claim that Jacobs' elk kill at the Flag Swamp, witnessed by him and Parmenter, actually occurred in 1835 or 1836 rather than in 1867, but Nelson may have wanted to maintain his status as the slayer of Pennsylvania's last elk in 1845. If so, Nelson had the same characteristics of the many old hunters who told their tales to A. O. Austin. "They were," Austin noted, "in the habit of making a good story of their exploits."

---

14. Samuel N. Rhoads, *Mammals of Pennsylvania and New Jersey*, 41.

15. Pennsylvania Game Commission website, "History of Elk in Pennsylvania"; Ira Parmenter's obituary, *New York Sun*, (no date given); Pennsylvania Genealogy Trails website, "Genealogy Trails Potter County Pennsylvania Obituaries and Death Notices."

A mother elk and her fawn. Two more posed elk that can be seen inside the Elk County Visitor Center, Elk County.

"A failing, I might add," he continued, "which is common to so many 'great, old men', that the world knows how to make allowance for it."[16]

If Jim Jacobs' trophy still exists today, it should be preserved in a museum and displayed as one of the last native elk shot in Pennsylvania. It is not a claim that was ever disputed by the state's hunters since it was a well-documented fact. However, those same sportsmen were not ready to accept the proclamation that elk were finally extinct in Pennsylvania from that time onward.

Dismayed by the extinction of the elk, the mountain lion, and other fine game species in Pennsylvania, the state's hunters in 1895 successfully lobbied for creation of a game commission to restore and protect wildlife. Since that time the commission has successfully brought deer, quail, wild turkey, and other game animals back into the forests where they were once so plentiful. Likewise, back in 1913, they also shipped a number of elk into Clinton, Clearfield, and other Pennsylvania counties on train cars from Yellowstone National Park in Wyoming.

16. Samuel N. Rhoads, *Mammals of Pennsylvania and New Jersey*, 39.

The restoration of the elk herd was a slow and uncertain process until when, in the 1960s, the Game Commission began concerted efforts to help the herd grow. Large areas were cleared in the forests so elk could browse on the tender shoots and plants that would eventually grow there. Remote meadows were planted with alfalfa and clover to divert the elk from farmers' fields, and this, too, helped the elk herd to finally flourish.

By 2001 the herd was estimated to be close to 600 in number, and a limited hunt was permitted throughout the Allegheny Highlands of Elk, Cameron, and Clearfield Counties. By 2018, the Pennsylvania Game Commission's continuing efforts to sustain and grow the elk herd had been so successful that they estimated that there were then approximately 1,000 animals.

If accurate, it made the state home to the largest elk herd east of the Rockies. Not a bad comeback for an animal whose extinction was once considered complete in Pennsylvania. Undoubtedly it would have stayed that way but for the stewards of the Pennsylvania wilds who wanted to restore the elk to their former glory.

NOTE: The author interviewed several old folks in Penns Valley, Centre County, back in the 1970s, who still recalled how hunters in 1913 killed elk along Elk Creek near Coburn and also through the Millheim Narrows. The animals had entered these areas as a result of the Game Commission's 1913 elk reintroduction program.

At first the elk had been kept in acclimation pens in the Big Lick and Old Mingle Hollow Game Preserves the Commission had set up in the White Mountains to the south. When the Game Commission felt that the elk had finally gotten used to their new environment, they released the animals in hopes they would once again become part of the ecosystem.

It was an ideal spot for the experiment, since even today the area is more or less an untamed wilderness where Rupp Mountain, Paddy Mountain, and Sawmill Mountain hide many secluded overlooks and impassible ravines, many of which are overgrown by crab apple and honey locust trees. The spiky thorns of the undergrowth, a tangle of wild raspberry and blackberry brambles, and of thorn and hazel bushes, make the areas all but impenetrable, and the dark hollows proved to be a safe haven for the elk.

Two bull elks with horns locked in their annual joust for mating rights.

Undoubtedly their ancestors had been here before if place-names can be trusted. Elk Gap is one such place up in the White Mountain Kettle, and Elk Creek flows off to the north at Coburn and into the Millheim Narrows. The creek was so-named, according to local tradition, because even though the elk were gone by the time the first white men entered the valley, those same early settlers were surprised at how many sets of elk antlers they could find lying near and along the creek bed. The name today is a reminder of how prevalent the animal once was throughout this section, and it is virtually all that is left to remind us of that fact.

Although the elk here in 1913 had been carefully acclimatized to their new home before being released, it turned out that the people in the area had not been acclimatized to the elk. Residents began to complain about having to throw stones at the elk to chase them out of their fields and gardens. It was illegal to shoot them, and farmers didn't like having to steer their teams off the road to get around elk that were so tame they weren't scared of humans.

They also became fed up with the elk's ongoing destruction of their crops, with the final straw being a newspaper article in the Philadelphia papers that made its way back into the mountains. The newspaper account, accompanied by pictures of the event, described a large elk barbecue held on Capitol Hill in Harrisburg. A Consensus quickly formed among the disgruntled Penn's Valley elk haters, who agreed "If the big shots on Capitol Hill can eat elk, so can we!"

From that point on local Penns Valley farmers and hunters took matters into their own hands. The farmers were fed up with the beasts because of crop destruction; the hunters, although badly misinformed, because they thought the elk would lead to a decrease in the deer herd here.

Many of them, risking the fines for doing so, shot elk on sight, sometimes reporting their kill to the Game Commission but most times not. Game wardens tried to maintain control, but the hunters were careful, and eventually there was only one old bull elk left and a very few females.

The old bull eventually seemed to become more and more of a problem, some believing it was because he was finding fewer and fewer female elk to mate with. At one point he even began to appear aggressive, frightening anyone who encountered it. Parents, in particular, were alarmed because the large wapiti would stand in the roadways traveled by their children on their way to and from school. Upon seeing them, or any other travelers, approaching, it would start to paw gravel as if preparing to charge. It was aggression that prompted many complaints to the Game Commission.

The Game Commission did come back and manage to shoot the annoying wapiti, and subsequent reports, accompanied by photographs of the dead animal, trumpeted it as the state's "last elk."

Nonetheless, men from Green Briar and Coburn kept on shooting until their kills, plus two consecutive hard winters, had reduced the elk herd to one old cow. The following spring one of the hunters saw this lone survivor swimming across Penns Creek just below the railroad bridge, and he shot it with a slug fired from a "Long Tom" shotgun. This was the last elk known to be killed here, and it met with an ignominious end, "floating down the creek," recalled one old-timer, "to the edging hole, where she hung on a rock!"[17]

---

17. Randall Steiger (born 1904), recorded November 5, 1980, June 4, 1982, and May 4, 1988; Blaine Malone (born 1903), interviewed October 23, 1980, and April 21, 1981.

CHAPTER XVI

A QUAINT REMINDER OF DAYS GONE BY

In *Pennsylvania Fireside Tales Volume VII* there is a chapter titled "War Whoop and Scalping Knife," in which is recalled the story of a colonial homestead in Union County exhibiting a relic that serves as a reminder of Pennsylvania's border Wars. The unusual memento was placed at the apex of the eastern side of the old stone house, new owners of the farm are told, to remind the builders of the place (Johannes and Susannah Sierer) of their divine deliverance from the hands of an Indian war party in 1779.

The Sierers told the story of their narrow escape to their children and grandchildren, who, in turn, passed it on to theirs, and it has come down to us today in that manner. The story also includes the reason that the Sierers had a stone mason chisel an image of an antique clock face onto a large stone that was used to complete the eastern wall of their mansion when it was built in 1795.

The image appears to have been modeled from the face of an old moving-moon-face tall case clock, complete with its roman numerals and its hour and minute hand set to a precise time. It is a curious decoration that invites a lot of speculation, until one knows the story behind it.

According to the tale that was told to me, and which is preserved in the aforementioned chapter, the Sierer family was alerted to the stealthily approaching war party by the barking of their family dog, which gave them enough time to escape and flee into the darkness of the nearby forest. It was a captivating story, but years later I found out that it was incomplete. There

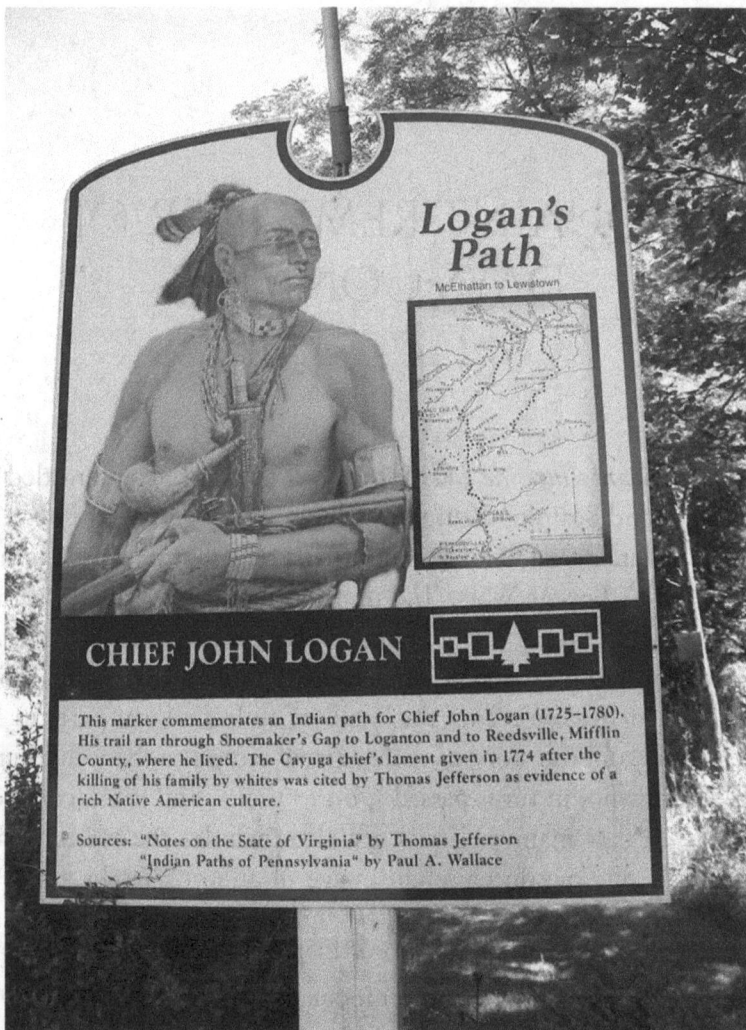

The Indian Path. Marker denoting the place where Cayuga Indian Chief Logan's path crossed through Shoemaker Gap in Clinton County and continued on to his village near present-day Reedsville, Mifflin County. This colorful memorial can be found near the quaint village of McElhattan, Clinton County, and near the Restless Oaks Restaurant where the Maguires provide delicious meals for customers. Also nearby is the historic "Restless Oaks" homestead of Henry W. Shoemaker who preserved many old-time central Pennsylvania legends.

The Sierer's original log cabin. Still standing and used as a family home today, this was the cabin in which the Sierer's were awakened and given timely warning of a stealthy Indian raiding party sneaking up on them.

were more details about that episode that only came to my attention when I visited the Sierer log cabin on a picture-taking trip during the summer of 2019.

I had knocked on the door of the modernized cabin to get permission to take some pictures. Mr. and Mrs. Will, the current owners, inquired why I wanted to do so, what story I had heard about the place, and where I had heard it. After answering their questions, they confirmed it was the correct one, whereupon they graciously invited me inside to take pictures of the remaining log wall of the Sierer cabin and of the Sierer fireplace as well.

Mrs. Will, as a fourth-generation descendant of some of the area's first settlers, knew a more-detailed version of the Sierer tale that had come down through many generations of her family. She confirmed that the barking of a dog had indeed saved the Sierers from the attacking warriors, but said the dog was not the family dog.

The Sierer cabin logs. The remaining logs of one wall of the Sierer's cabin as they look today inside the historic structure, which is located near present-day Buffalo Crossroads, Union County.

It turns out that the day before the attack, Mr. Sierer had come back to the cabin after a hard day's work in his fields only to find that their neighbor had brought his daughters a present that day. The present was a puppy that was so cute and cuddly that the young girls had fallen in love with it at once. Johannes Sierer, on the other hand, was less than pleased.

After taking one look at the dog. the tired farmer told his family that it would have to be returned the next day. "I've got too many mouths to feed as it is," he railed, and "I cannot afford another." So the Sierer sisters went to bed with tears in their eyes, but it was that same dog that proved to be an excellent watch dog and whose barking woke the family that night to warn them of approaching Indians.

And it is the time that it did so that is memorialized on the clock face that can still be seen on the homestead built by the Sierers sixteen years later when they had become prosperous enough to afford more upscale housing.

The Sierers' safe haven. The field of rye into which the Sierers escaped was located where the trees and clearing in the left side of the picture are today, Union County.

The other piece of the story that the Wills were able to add to my version of the tale is that, when they escaped from the cabin, the Sierers did not flee into the dark forest to the south, but rather into a field of fall-planted rye that was in a field right behind the cabin.

It had grown to a height of about three feet, which was not that high, but it was apparently high enough that the warring savages could not find the family. Either that or they thought the Sierers had not been there to start with. In either case, the warriors left, but not before vandalizing the Sierer cabin as a display of their frustration in having to leave without the scalps that they had hoped to claim.

INTERESTING HISTORICAL CORROBORATION

For those who are skeptical about the account of the Sierer family and their dog hiding from Indian marauders in a nearby rye field without being discovered because the dog remained uncharacteristically quiet, the following account from Westmoreland County may prove convincing:

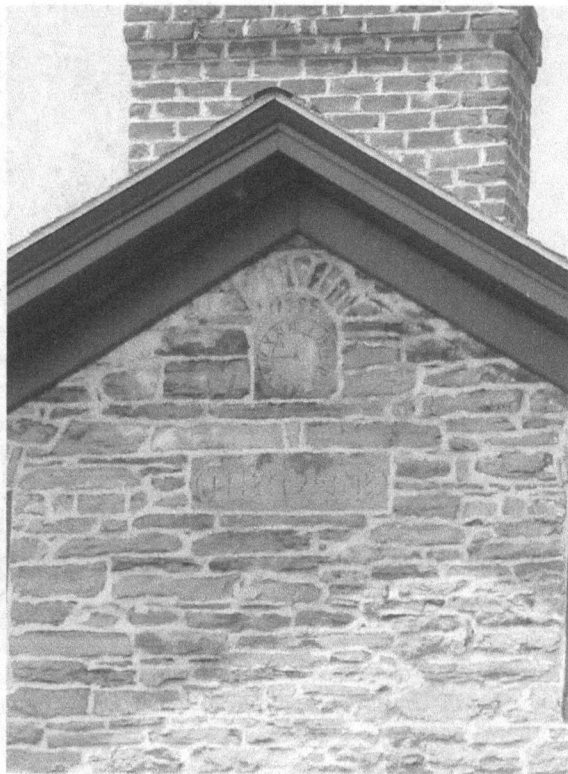

Clock face on the Sierer Homestead, Buffalo Township, Union County.

"The summer of 1782 was the gloomiest in our pioneer history," writes historian John N. Boucher in his *History of Westmoreland County* (Volume 1, Chapter 12, pp. 177–78). He also notes that the infamous Indian attack on Hannastown occurred July 13, 1782, the day after an ambush occurred on a nearby wedding party, he describes as follows:

"As the Indian troubles accumulated the pioneers became more and more united, until the summer of 1782 they nearly all lived in forts or blockhouses or in close proximity."

Despite the constant threat of marauding war parties, the pioneers were determined to carry on with their lives as normally as possible, including cementing the bonds of true love. As Boucher notes, "Love, like wild violets" continued to "blossom in the wilderness," and so on July 12, 1782, a wedding ceremony took place at Miller's Block-house near Hannastown,

Westmoreland County. The event drew many people to it, such ceremonies being few and far between at that period. There were many young men and women there, and "there had been dancing to the tune of a fiddle, and playing and great glee among the guests, as was the custom in that day."

"Everything went off merrily until about the middle of the afternoon, when suddenly, like a peal of thunder from a cloudless sky, the war whoop burst upon their ears, and a band of savages rushed into their midst.

"Among those who escaped by flight was the daughter of Judge Hanna. She was taken on horseback by Samuel Findley, a pack-horse driver, and carried to the country, and thus escaped.

"A young man who had hastened to Miller's to give the alarm, in making his escape took with him a child. He was very soon pursued by three or four Indians who were gaining on him, although he could easily have distanced them in a foot race had he not been burdened by the child. This race was kept up for some time, and the young man's strength was rapidly waning.

"Fortunately, he came to a thick growth of underbrush, and beyond it was a high rail fence which bordered a field of uncut rye. He passed through the brush, mounted the fence, and jumped from the top of it as far into the rye field as he could. While in the brush and crossing the fence he was out of sight of the Indians. Then he lay down on the ground with the child, which fortunately kept quiet. The Indians came up and passed him without discovering him. They soon returned and looked more closely, but did not find him. Their time was necessarily brief, and they left with many mutterings of disgust."

CHAPTER XVII

GHOSTS: UP CLOSE AND PERSONAL!

Fear of the dark and what it conceals seems to be imprinted upon mankind's subconscious mind. The obvious reason for that, I think, is because of the darkness in which our ancestors had to live, even just a hundred years ago. Imagine if you will that you are a young child living in an ancient farmhouse and every night you have to ascend a long winding staircase to your bedroom. The massive house has no electric lights since electricity has not yet made it to this remote section of the countryside, and so you are carrying a small kerosene lamp to light your way.

Each step you take causes movement of the lantern you hold and weird shadows dance on the stairs in front of you. All the while strange creaks and groans emanate from the steps upon which you tread, and from walls and floors all around you. Your imagination begins to run wild, and you begin to wonder if maybe there are such things as ghosts after all!

Low toneless moans that sound like echoes coming from the depths of a cold dark crypt; bony fingers clasping the back of the neck; sharp pinching or painful scratching on the upper back or on the arms; icy temperatures that penetrate into the body's core. These are all sensations reported by those who claim to have come into the presence of ghostly beings, and although I've personally never experienced such things, I've always been curious about whether ghostly phenomena like this are fact or fancy.

It was this same curiosity that inspired me to set myself up like an investigative reporter of sorts to decide if any of the stories I collected for my *Pennsylvania Fireside Tales* books have a basis in fact, or are nothing more than tall tales—products from the imaginations of gifted storytellers. The major difficulty with that approach when it comes to ghosts, however, is how do you verify something that appears to be outside the boundaries of the natural world? How do you get "up close and personal" with a ghost?

The answer, of course, is to go where they "live," visit the spots they call home. I've never been committed to the idea that ghosts are something that require supernatural explanations. Instead, I've come to the conclusion that although I believe the phenomenon is real, there are probably natural explanations for it; a part of the natural world we just do not yet understand.

Otherwise, I would have to resort to the maxim that "extraordinary claims require extraordinary proof." It was natural for me, then, having been educated as a scientist and a mathematician, to want to investigate the phenomenon as much as possible. It was also natural for me to find ways to do so as scientifically as possible, including accompanying some select "ghost hunter" groups during a few of their on-site investigations.

After all, I realized, the more committed these groups are, the more likely they are to take a logical, state-of-the-art approach when attempting to find ghosts; the more determined they are to debunk any evidence, whether from video, audio, or photographic sources, no matter how compelling it might seem. I was therefore selective in the groups I chose to accompany.

There was one in particular that appealed to me, not only because they were right next door, but also because of their commitment to finding the undisputed truth to the question of what, if anything, lies behind the curtain that seems to separate us from this world and the next; what can be done to penetrate that dark veil that seems so impenetrable? My interest in working with this group was also prompted by the fact that they wanted to investigate some of the more sensational haunted places I had written about in my books.

There were certainly a few such places I had discovered over the years, but many did not lend themselves to an on-site investigation. In some cases, the ghostly visitations that supposedly happened at these dreary spots did not occur at any set date or time; they were random and relatively unpredictable. In other cases, the exact spots where the ghosts were seen are no longer known or have been deliberately obscured by families wanting to disassociate themselves from lurid tales about the ghostly realm.

A tale that falls into this latter category would have to be one collected by early folklorist Alfred Shoemaker, who wrote about it in his weekly "Local Folklore" newspaper column in the *Lancaster Intelligencer Journal* in the 1920s. Here in one such column he recalled a striking episode that was related to him by one Amos Yerger of Lititz.

The place where this unusual tale unfolded was not revealed in Shoemaker's article and so it is not a candidate for any of my up-close-and-personal type investigations, but I include it here because it reveals yet another type of superstition once prevalent in the Pennsylvania Dutch regions of the state. It also reveals, I think, how such superstitions could undoubtedly influence peoples' perceptions.

According to Alfred Shoemaker's article, old Pennsylvania Dutchman Yerger claimed that black cats were always associated with *Hexerei* (evil spells) and *Umglick* (bad luck). His strong support for that belief came from a passage in Pennsylvania Dutch Scripture, where it states that *"Un der Solomon Spricht, schwatze katze mausen nicht"* (and Solomon sayeth, black cats do not catch mice)!

On a more personal note, the old gentlemen said that his belief in the unnatural nature of black cats was not based on just this passage of Scripture, but also on a personal experience he had when he was just a young lad working as a hired hand on a local farm. He recalled that the barn and farmyard were overrun with cats and there was a large black one that was particularly troublesome. So, one day the farmer told young Yerger to chloroform the feline and then chop off its head on the stump in the chicken yard that was used as a chopping block to butcher chickens.

The young man reluctantly completed the assigned task, but his conscience troubled him afterwards, until his guilt seemed to overwhelm him one night about two weeks later, on a Friday the 13th.

"Es waar im dunkel rum muun," (it was in the dark of the moon—an expression that indicates a period when the moon is not shining or when it is obscured) was the way Yerger began his story when he told Shoemaker how he arose that night to close the tobacco shed shutters he had forgotten to shut that day.

By this time the night was very dark, and a thunderstorm had blown in, so the sleepy lad was in a hurry to set up the long ladder he used to reach the shutters. In his haste he inadvertently walked under the ladder, and just as he did there was a bright flash of lightning which illuminated the nearby family cemetery where he had buried the remains of the cat.

At first, he was dumbstruck by the horror that the lightning revealed, but he could not take his eyes away from what he thought was the black cat trotting toward the cemetery. As if that would not have been bad enough, the old man also claimed that "*Sie hot ihr kopp im maul katt!*" (The cat carried its head in its mouth!)

There were other tales like this that proved frustratingly hard for me to pin down exactly where they occurred, but it was equally frustrating to know the exact place where a haunting supposedly occurs but to not know when its ghosts may reveal themselves. This situation is typical of most hauntings, of course, but there are two in particular that bear mentioning because each one offers a different perspective on the problem.

One of the more enticing tales that has this slippery quality to it, is that of the ghost train that some say they occasionally hear clattering over the abandoned railroad bed of the Williamsport and North Branch Railroad, along old Route 220, near the town of Glen Mawr in Lycoming County. No trains have been through here since the railroad filed for bankruptcy in 1937 and then tore up the tracks the following year, but sometimes late at night local residents say they hear a sound like that of a train moving along steel rails. They also claim that the sound is accompanied by what appears to be the red glow of an old-time railroad signaling lantern light moving along down the tracks as well. Intriguing as the story may be, no one has an explanation for the phenomena, and it would no doubt take multiple night-time vigils to investigate it since it does not occur regularly, nor at all during the daytime.[1]

There is another supposedly haunted place which offers yet another dilemma to those who wish to investigate such sites. Here the spectral inhabitant prefers to remain at rest and manages to do so until it is provoked. At least that's what the popular legend contends. On the other hand, there are those who say the whole story is nothing but a fabrication

---

1. Thomas T. Taber III, *Muncy Valley Lifeline, the Life and Times of the Williamsport and North Branch Railroad*, 57.

to start with. Nonetheless, at least there is a tombstone here that confirms there once was a person with the name recalled in the legend. Moreover, the dates on that tombstone coincide with the time period during which the events in the tale supposedly occurred.

On a little-visited hilltop in the Muncy Hills near Millville, Columbia County, the tombstone of Kate Ella Vandine sits in a remote cemetery adjacent to the Emmanuel Lutheran Church. Engraved on her large memorial are her birth (1862) and death (17 Feb. 1881) dates, which show that she was only 19 years old when she died.

The reason for her untimely death has been a subject of debate since the late 1800s, and the older generations in the area have always contended that the story is not a recent fabrication, but has been told and retold since that time. Consequently, if the story has any factual basis whatsoever, the question has to be raised as to why the young lady is buried in the church's graveyard at all.

Suicides or executed witches, when all's said and done, never got buried in hallowed ground! Today the church is popularly known as Katy's Church, and the woeful tale of Katy Vandine has circulated around the old chapel since she died here under uncertain circumstances. What is suggestive, however, is the fact that her name is attached to this little church in the wildwood. Something must have happened to her here that indelibly stamped her name upon it.

The first account that claims to explain this connection says that Katy fell in love with and was engaged to a local boy who went off to do his patriotic duty during the Civil War. In his absence Katy bought a beautiful new wedding dress in anticipation of the matrimonial celebration she knew would take place when her fiancé returned.

Sadly, that happy occasion was not to be. Katy was devasted upon learning that her dashing soldier had been killed during a battle somewhere in the southland. It's related that she was so devastated that she put on her beautiful wedding dress, slipped a noose around her neck, and hanged herself from a limb of one of the large ancient trees that still can be seen standing next to the church today.

There is another, even more damning, rendition of the tale that says Katy hanged herself here because of shame and the accompanying ostracism of all those she knew. In this case the story goes that the young woman was seduced and gotten pregnant by an older man. As an unmarried pregnant woman, she could not take the scorn heaped upon her by the community. Finally in her despair she decided the only way out of her situation was to take her own life.

A third permutation of the same tale claims that, in order to save his own reputation, the married man who had gotten Katy pregnant started the rumor that Katy was a witch who had bewitched him and forced him to have sex. In this account it's said that locals believed the rumors and forced Katy from her bed one dark night and hanged her from the ancient tree in order to rid the community of her evil influences.

It is from these accounts that the belief arose that the old cemetery was haunted by Katy's restless spirit. The explanations as to why she haunted the cemetery were widely circulated and tended to get increasingly more lurid as they spread. Those tales have lingered on, and even today there are some who claim they've seen Katy's shimmering white spirit flitting through the cemetery in her wedding dress. Moreover, others even avow they've heard her weird cries coming from inside the church late at night, have seen blood dripping from the church's windows, or have seen the image of a noose hanging from one of the limbs of the trees in the graveyard.

There are even more fantastic claims, including ones that state that on nights of a harvest moon, if you stand on or urinate on her grave, her angry spirit will appear. So, are any of the tales about Katy Vandine and the haunted church grounds true? Debunkers of the tales might refer to a claim by a Vandine descendant who thought that the Katy of the legends was "also known as Catherine, and a member of the church who lived to be 87 years old"[2] On the other hand, as previously stated, the tombstone for Katy Van Dine in Katy's Church Cemetery has her birth date as 1862 and her death occurring in 1881, making her 19 years old when she died. There are no other Cathy, Catherine, or Katherine Van Dine's buried there. Obviously the Catherine Van Dine mentioned by her descendants was not the same as the nineteen-year-old Katy Van Dine buried in the cemetery. So the legend lives on!

Of course, it is macabre stories like these have attracted those adventuresome souls who wish to encounter Katy's ghost. However, always frustrated

2. "The Haunted Legend of Katy's Church in Millville," NorthCentralPA newsletter, northcentralpa.com.

by their failures to conjure up any spirits, they resort to vandalism, with the takeaways from their ghost hunts being heavy fines for trespassing and for destruction of church property.

It is this last tale that provides a nice transition into the up-close-and-personal investigations I decided to do myself. One of the most popular ghost tales I wrote about in my *Pennsylvania Fireside Tales* books (see *Volume I*), was that of "The Mournful Ghost of Swamp Church." The story is very similar to that of Katy of Katy's Church, with the difference being that the Swamp Church ghost is supposedly consistent in its appearances; always appearing at midnight on every third of May. It was therefore for this reason that my ghost-hunter friends from Spring Hill Paranormal Investigators in Bellefonte persuaded me to accompany them to the church one May 3, in 2019.

We arrived there early to give them time to set up their cameras and recording equipment so all would be in place and ready when midnight arrived. We had gotten permission and the key to enter the church from its current owners, and so we went inside and began setting up right away.

It was a cool spring night with thick clouds of fog swirling around the church and in the nearby forest and fields, thereby making perfect conditions for a "ghost hunt!" Moreover, as if to enhance the feeling of this uncanny atmosphere, a number of spring peepers, who made their home in boggy ground along the Swamp Church Road, began to serenade us with their weird notes.

The sad peeps of the small frogs made our surroundings seem even more unnatural that night. Accordingly, by the time midnight came and all equipment was in place, our senses seemed even more attuned to the supernatural.

The midnight fog had intensified by the time I decided to walk up to the end of the Swamp Church Road to take some pictures. After doing so, I began walking back toward the church through the thick mist. Then, as I felt its clammy dampness on the back of my neck, I began to wonder what it was concealing. With the dense clouds of fog swirling around me, I began to think that it must have been nights like this that prompted Sir Arthur Conan Doyle to so vividly describe his famous detective enveloped by a similar mist.

Doyle often imagined Sherlock Holmes walking down the smog-choked streets of Victorian London. As Holmes walked along, he often passed under ornate gas street lights. The streets were so dark that the only evidence that the lamps were there at all was the diffuse yellow glow of their lamps trying to penetrate the thick mist that filled every alley and corner.

The iconic detective's surroundings, I imagined, would have seemed as surreal to him as our surroundings at the Swamp Church felt to me this night. The beams of our flashlights were no match for the blanket of fog that enveloped us, and they created a diffuse and ghostly white radiance that cast weird shadows across the roadway. Once I got back to the church, however, I began to relax, until we realized we had company.

When we saw a number of flashlights coming down the road toward the church, we waited until we were approached by a group of high school kids, who had come to do their own investigation. The boys and girls had been told the story of the church's ghost by one of their high school teachers and they were anxious to see if they could see the black apparition themselves.

We shooed them away, even though we found them to be a very respectful and honest group, and they left in disappointment. Likewise, in the end, we, like those kids, had to admit defeat as well. We experienced no supernatural events that night, nor were there, we later determined, any such events recorded on our video or audio equipment. Nonetheless, that did not deter us from wanting to investigate the other ghost sites we had planned to visit, at the specific times when the ghosts at these places supposedly made themselves known.

So on yet another night, following a bleak December day, we braved the cold winds of mid-winter and trekked up to the Rock Cemetery along Shiloh Road in Benner Township near State College. After crunching along the frozen mud of a tractor path covered by a light skiff of snow, we finally reached the burial ground.

By that time, we were chilled to the bone, since the temperature was just below the freezing point, and the night winds were forcefully swaying the trees. Although the night was pitch black, the light covering of snow seemed to provide an eerie illumination of its own, enough for us to see the steps leading up and over the stone wall surrounding the tombstones within.

Once inside this small "God's half acre" we began taking pictures, trying to stay occupied while we determinedly awaited the coming of the witching hour. Our presence did not go unnoticed, however, as a group of owls sitting in a copse of trees on a nearby hilltop began voicing their dismal songs, perhaps expressing displeasure at our nighttime intrusion. In fact, their weird notes, which accompanied the light flurry of snow swirling in the cold gusts of wind, heightened our tensions and seemed to enhance the supernatural feel of this lonely spot.

It was New Year's Eve, and midnight is the time that the "Weeping Ghost" of Rock Cemetery, as I like to call her, supposedly appears on her gravesite and sits there weeping. The reason, we had read, was because she mourns for the proper burial she never received, and she is also grieving over her untimely death. At least that's what the story that's been handed down for decades about this place declares to be the truth.

The young lady buried here, according to the tale (see the chapter titled "Ghosts of the Graveyard" in the author's *Pennsylvania Fireside Tales Volume VII* for the complete account), was hastily interred at this spot because she died of a horrible disease that was spreading like wildfire among her fellow villagers. Those folks, in their haste to protect themselves by burying her and leaving as quickly as possible, did not read her any last rites. Nor did they mark her burial place with a solid gravestone, instead only carving the words "Died at Night" on a pine board they nailed to a stake which they later pounded into the ground at the spot where she was to find eternal rest.

We could not find any such epitaph on any of the weather-worn and sunken gravestones in the cemetery this night, and the wooden marker, if it ever existed, has since rotted away. Despite that lack of evidence, the tale claims that the young woman's restless spirit still clings to this spot. We therefore were hoping to at least be rewarded for braving the elements this cold dark night in winter by a visitation; some unmistakable manifestations of her presence.

Our preceding research on the burial ground indicated that a virulent pestilence had spread through here in 1821, leading to many deaths. Nonetheless, the earliest graves to be found here today were of those interred in

Midnight view of the Rock Cemetery where the weeping ghost is said to appear. No ghost this night but some orbs in the photo!

the 1830s, and the youngest of these was for seventeen-year-old Elizabeth Heverley who died in 1831. We therefore focused our cameras on her resting place, but not at the expense of the graveyard's other tombstones, taking many pictures of the entire cemetery.

In the end we were to be disappointed here as well. We left with no photographic or audio evidence of anything out of the ordinary, despite staying here until well after midnight.

Our next ghost investigation, also near State College in Centre County, led us to a mysterious woodland where, many locals believe, lurks the infamous "Black Ghost of Scotia" (see the author's *Pennsylvania Fireside Tales Volume II* and his *Pennsylvania Fireside Ghost Tales* for the story behind this often-seen revenant and for accounts of those who have personally witnessed it.)

The ghost of Bert Delige has appeared and reappeared in "the Barrens," as it's locally referred to, numerous times since he committed a murder here in October of 1911, and its appearance always coincides with the anniversary date of the day he was hanged for his bloody crime.

The author in Rock Cemetery celebrating New Year's Eve with a walk among the tombstones (Photo courtesy of Spring Hill Paranormal Investigators.)

The Barrens is a spot often frequented by hikers, runners, hunters, and fisherman during the day since deer, bears, smaller wildlife, and pleasant hiking paths can be found here. Come nightfall the dark forest of the Barrens becomes a place so still and so silent that even its woodland residents seem to sense that something evil is lurking in its shadows. And that was the feeling we got, when we got out of our car to begin our investigation.

It was a cloudy afternoon in late October when the sun was just beginning to sink in the western sky. We looked with appreciation upon the magnificent sunset on the horizon while following a path along a cornfield next to the Scotia Barrens forest. A strong night wind suddenly roared into our faces and began to rattle the dead leaves that still clung to the skeletal tree branches. That same wind also caused the dried stalks of corn next to us to rattle as well, and those noises, along with our darkening surroundings, caused our imaginations to run wild.

We thought the rattling of a skeleton's bones might sound the same. As those noises became louder, our minds began to race, wondering if the noises made by the wind might be a warning from ghosts that were lurking in the woods to our left. Maybe they were agitated by our presence here at this hour.

But no spirits came to the fore that night, and when we walked back out the way we had come, the woods suddenly became silent; the night wind suddenly died, leaving us wondering if the spirits here were placated when they saw us leaving! On the other hand, we had to wonder if our timing had been right. October was the month Delige had murdered Mrs. Baudis, but maybe we needed to come back on April 25, the anniversary of Delige's hanging, and try again. That, we agreed to do.

Our final attempt to find evidence of the spirit world took us to Union County. Here, along a little-traveled and darkly-shadowed mountain thoroughfare, is supposedly the hiding place of the ghost I like to call the Luminescent Ghost of White Deer Valley (see the chapter titled "Moonlight and Deathly Shadows" in the author's *Pennsylvania Fireside Ghost Tales* for the story of this spirit and how it appeared before some Lock Haven University students one night).

The gravel mountain road known as the White Deer Pike traverses White Deer Valley, and anyone passing through here at night will no doubt regard it as an almost God-forsaken place. There are very few houses or camps along this stretch of roadway, and so it is the perfect spot for a lingering spirit who wants to remain undisturbed. My ghost-hunting friends and I were hoping that this would not be the case this night; hoping that the apparition of the beautiful woman that seems to be inescapably tied to this place would show itself.

It was a gloomy night in late October, with a light rainfall, when we turned off Route 80 at the Mile Run exit, then left onto the White Deer Turnpike. There were still some twilight hours left and so we could appreciate the multi-colored leaves clinging to the branches of the trees along the roadway. The branches were mostly bare, having been swept clean by the strong winds of early fall, but those that remained lent an autumnal atmosphere to the steady rain that made them glisten in our car's headlights.

We pulled off the road and sat there awhile until complete darkness had finally fallen upon us. As we waited, we could see gossamer clouds of mist beginning to rise from the old turnpike and in the woods that surrounded us. It seemed like a perfect night for a ghost hunt, and so when

The Rock Cemetery at New Year's Eve in lantern light. Elizabeth Heverley's tomb at midnight. (Photo courtesy of Spring Hill Paranormal Investigators.)

darkness finally came, we began to drive back and forth on the roadway, looking for the luminescence that would reveal her presence.

Perhaps it was the rain, or maybe the timing wasn't correct, but whatever the case may be, we once again had to admit defeat. Nonetheless, we vowed we would try again someday; agreed we would come back when the weather was better, thinking that maybe the beautiful ghost would be more likely to appear in weather that was fair rather than foul.

What then are we to conclude from our investigations? We found no ghosts at the spots where they supposedly exist, nor did we find any evidence to support claims that ghosts are something more than phantasmagorical imaginings.

In other words, from our brief investigations we cannot staunchly refute the oft-repeated claims of scholarly skeptics. These scholars, along with the general public, have often belittled those who hold supernatural beliefs about ghosts. They say that those beliefs can be attributed to ignorance and even to profound stupidity.

On the other hand, those same skeptics, in my opinion, exhibit a different yet equally profound folly, that is akin to the folly they attribute to those they criticize. And that irrationality is their refusal to accept the fact that even the most fantastic-sounding phenomenon is worthy of scientific study when it is experienced by so many people for so long. That there is, in fact, potential for gain in scientific knowledge when empirical folk wisdom is not merely discounted as faulty observations of untutored minds. And therein lies the allure for those who continue their quest to experience ghosts "up close and personal."

CHAPTER XVIII

MORE LAST PANTHER TALES

It's surprising to me how nineteenth and early twentieth century stories of Pennsylvania's mountain lions have survived, especially since these great predators were essentially wiped out in that same time period. Just recently in this current year (2024), I was told another old-time account and discovered yet another in a newspaper chronicle, both of which were among the most interesting of these types of tales I'd ever come across. It shows that, unlike the stories from the days when wolves still plagued travelers and farmers' livestock in our mountains, the old-time mountain lion stories have managed to survive longer.

Nonetheless, those mountain lion tales are not that common, and they are scattered sporadically across Pennsylvania today. That's unsurprising given the fact that the mountain lion, or panther, as the original settlers called it, was not that prevalent statewide. In Potter County, for example, historians have noted that in the early nineteenth century, "The wildlife in this area was fairly plentiful in those early times. The elk, deer and bear were present. The panther was rarely found but several are recorded as being killed and the bounty collected."[1]

That statement was confirmed by E. N. Woodcock, who was born at Lymansville, Potter County, in 1844. This venerable hunter and trapper of the Black Forest country and beyond, recalled that as a boy "The woods extended to the very door of my father's house and deer were more numerous than sheep in the fields at the present day. Bear were also quite plentiful, and wolves were to be found in considerable numbers in certain

---

1. *Historical Sketches of Potter County*, 10.

Nelson and Mary Gardner. He was the slayer of the last panther in Elk County.

localities. Panthers were much talked of and occasionally one would be killed by some hunter or trapper."[2]

Mrs. Rebecca Reeder, born in 1808 near present-day Carmel, Northumberland County, recalled how plentiful game was in that area as well; and how, in one year, her father "shot forty deer, six bears, and three panthers, besides smaller game."[3]

From these descriptions it seems clear that the panther was an elusive quarry, especially as the nineteenth century drew to a close. For similar descriptions and tales that confirm this statement, see the chapter titled "Stragglers" in the author's *Pennsylvania Fireside Tales Volume IV.*

2. E. N. Woodcock, *Fifty Years a Hunter and Trapper*, 55.
3. H. C. Bell, *History of Northumberland County, Pennsylvania*, 656.

W. J. McKnight also commented on the scarcity of the panther in early northwestern Pennsylvania by noting "The largest carnivorous beast was the panther. After the advent of white men into this wilderness panthers were not common."[4] Despite or because of its scarcity, the mountain lion was a hunter's ultimate trophy of the chase, and several of these nimrods became known for their indefatigable pursuit of those trophies. In Jefferson County, for example, the Longs and Vastbinders were among that group.

On one occasion it's recorded that Jackson Long, son of northwestern Pennsylvania's "king hunter" Bill Long, "entered a panther's den in Jefferson County and shot the animal by the light of its glowing eyes." Similarly, it's noted that "In 1833, Jacob and Peter Vastbinder found a panther's den on Boone's Mountain, now Elk County. They killed one, the dogs killed two, and these hunters caught a cub, which they kept for a year and sold it to a showman."[5]

When a young man, the king hunter once fell asleep after dressing a deer he had shot along the North Fork. Covering himself with the pelt, he awoke to find himself covered by sticks and leaves. Knowing that a female panther had covered him in this way thinking he would be food for her cubs, he also knew she would soon be returning with those cubs.

"He therefore prepared a pitch-pine fagot, lit it, and hid the burning fagot under the bank and awaited the coming of the panther. In a short time after this preparation was completed the animal returned with her cubs, and when she was within about thirty feet of him, Long thrust his torch up and out, and when it blazed up brightly the panther gave out a yell and ran away."[6]

There was a settler up in northeastern Pennsylvania's Pike County whose escape from a panther did not go quite so easily. Levi Labar, born in 1823 in Pike County, was a Civil War veteran, serving as a private with other Pike County men in Company B, 151st Regiment. Having seen action in some notable battles, including Gettysburg, Labar came home and settled in Palmyra Township, married Hannah Smith in 1866, and raised seven children with her.

It was after his marriage that Labar had an encounter with a mountain lion that not only went down in the history books, but which also

4. W. J. McKnight, *Pioneer Outline History of Northwestern Pennsylvania*, 119.
5. Ibid.
6. Ibid, 158.

made newspapers all over the northeast and as far west as Illinois. His story was published again on May 14, 2018, in the *Tri-County Independent* of Honesdale, Wayne County, PA.

The article, written by Managing Editor Peter Becker, was titled "Levi Labar's Story." The editor claimed it was Labar's personal account, with details combined from "different published reports." The story ran as follows:

A BATTLE WITH A WILD CAT

Levi Labar, of Purdytown, had a terrible fight with a catamount in his bedroom the night of March 17, 1884. The animal entered through a large windowpane which had been broken and was covered with a piece of cloth nailed to the sash. About midnight, after Labar [*sic*] had gone to bed, he heard a strange noise in the room.

On jumping up to make an investigation a sharp, unearthly yell was given by the wildcat, which made the very air jingle.

Labor seized a piece of wood, and without stopping to make a light, attacked the animal, which at once sprung upon his shoulders.

Labor shook it off and gave a stunning blow with his club. For fifteen minutes the conflict raged fiercely, the brute leaping from wall to wall, clinging to the paper with its sharp claws and then bounding upon its opponent, screeching with fury, and with eyes shining like coals of fire.

At last Labar dealt the cat a death blow just as it was about to leap on his head from the top of an open door. The animal was one of the largest ever seen in that section of country. It measured eight feet [another newspaper said six feet] from the tip of its nose to the end of its tail.

Labar was severely lacerated about the face and arms.

Where did they go? Surely the catamount didn't want to be in the house any more than Labar wanted it there. We can only imagine that the window was fixed in short order.

According to the U.S. Fish and Wildlife Service (USFWS), the Eastern Cougar subspecies, which once populated most of the eastern states, disappeared from this range at least 70 years ago. The panther is well known in the western states, and there is a small population in Florida.

Reports of sightings, however, have lingered through the decades, although substantive evidence of a breeding population has been lacking. According to the USFWS, cougars that have been seen back in their ancestral range are either escaped or released from captivity, or in rare cases, have wandered from the west.

USFWS states that most eastern cougars were killed out of fear for human and livestock safety and were victims of massive deforestation and over-harvesting white-tailed deer, the cougar's primary prey.

In his 1880 book, Goodrich wrote, "The marvelous stories sometimes told about bears, wolves and panthers, without provocation aggressively attacking men, women, or children should be received with many grains of allowance. That fear of man, seemingly impressed on the brute creation by a Higher Power, restrains them from committing any such violence."

Tell that to the cougar that entered Labar's bedroom. We wonder if Levi Labar had read Goodrich's book!

That's probably one of the scariest panther tales I've ever collected, but just the sounds of a panther's cries were sometimes enough to send chills up the spines of those who heard them, as this next story will attest. It's a tale I just heard during July of 2024, and so it can claim the distinction of being the latest I've collected from an oral source. It has never, to the best of my knowledge, ever been recorded on the printed page before.

Preserved in the memories of a parish church in Centre County is the story about one of its earliest pastors during the late nineteenth century. The young man must have had the stamina of an Olympian and a wife with the patience of Job, given the trek he had to make every Sunday.

His parish consisted of two United Brethren churches in the small communities of Valley View and Unionville, which were close as the crow flies, but widely separated when it came to the roads that needed to be traversed to get to each one any given Sunday morning.

The young minister was charged with giving a Sunday service at each of his parish churches as scheduling permitted, and when giving a service at his Unionville church he had to travel a steep and winding road over Bald Eagle Mountain from Valley View to get there. The stoic cleric must neither have owned nor have been provided with a horse and buggy for his trips, because it's recalled he had to walk to both churches whenever holding services.

James McCurdy. Also born in 1816, he was a contemporay of Nelson Gardner and was another wolf and panther hunter in the wilds of Elk County.

It had to be a daunting task, and so he must have been a dedicated man of God to provide that level of worship to his parishioners. Moreover, his wife's dedication had to be just as strong since she would always accompany him on his Sunday walks. At least she did so until something occurred one dark winter Sunday when they were returning from their Unionville service and were descending the roadway down the Bald Eagle Mountain.

On that particular afternoon, the wife told her husband that she thought she heard a baby's cries. He told her to ignore it, that it was "just the wind." A little further on she told him once again that she thought she heard a baby's cries. However, once again, he told her that it was just the wind. When she claimed to hear the cries a third time; he again dismissed it as the wind. However, after reaching the safety of their home, he confessed to her that what she had heard was a panther's cries, and that it no doubt was following them in hopes of making one of them its next meal.

The lady then and there vowed that she would never walk that way again, and maybe the pastor decided at that point that he needed to carry a rifle on that portion of his Sunday sojourns. History does not say one way or another, but there are those who aver that the panther screams heard by the minister's wife may have been nothing more than the wind after all.[7]

---

7. Cheryl Houser, interviewed July 18, 2024.

Along a wintry Bald Eagle Mountain Road. It was along this road that the minister's wife heard the panther's cries, which she thought were the sounds of a baby crying.

That venerable Potter County hunter and trapper E. N. Woodcock had his own opinion about the sounds people claimed were made by a panther. In a chapter (#26) titled "The Screech of the Panther" in his classic *Fifty Years a Hunter and Trapper*, Woodcock, born in 1844, stated that he firmly believed that many of the screeches people claimed were those made by a panther could instead by attributed to screech owls.

"And still to this day," Woodcock began in an article published in the *Hunter, Trader, and Trapper* magazine of 1903, "there is occasionally a person who reports of hearing that terrible screech of the panther here in old Potter, notwithstanding that there has not been a panther killed in the county for upwards of fifty years, though twice within fifty years I have been frightened nearly out of my boots by that terrible screech."[8]

He goes on to describe the two instances where he was badly frightened by screeches coming from just over his head. The first occurred when he was walking along a heavily timbered roadway to his hunting camp and the

8. E. N. Woodcock, *Fifty Years a Hunter and Trapper*, 244 ff.

second when he was sitting in his deer stand overlooking a salt lick often frequented by deer.

In both those cases Woodcock discovered that a screech owl had silently alighted nearby, within several feet in the deer stand encounter, and both times had frightened him so badly as to take his breath away.

He reinforces his claims by stating that he often heard his father, a staid Black Forest woodsman in his own right, say "he never heard any kind of a noise that he thought came from a panther—and panthers were plentiful in those sections in those days. Father laughed at the idea of the panther screaming, when he heard people telling of hearing them." Based on his father's claims and on his personal experiences, Woodcock seems to have firmly concluded that "The screech of the panther I believe to be all imagination."[9]

Nonetheless, he seems to have been ambivalent about the matter as just five paragraphs before this claim, he contradicts himself when he writes "However, regardless of what my father and other early settlers of this section, who were not possessed of strong imaginary minds have told me, as well as my own personal experience, I have evidence that the panther does scream and scream terribly too."

Woodcock then cites two experiences related to him by his neighbor, who worked in Clearfield County hauling supplies for a lumber camp there. His neighbor, Mike Green, recalled that in both cases he was out on the road late at night hauling supplies that included several quarters of fresh beef.

On the first night, Green heard the screams of a panther in the woods skirting the road. He narrowly escaped an attack by whipping his team into a gallop and driving rapidly into camp. The panther, recalled Green, followed him the whole way "screaming at every jump."[10]

There was a second time, a few nights later, when the panther attacked again. He first heard its screams, which prompted him to whip his team at a faster pace. Then when close to the camp, the panther, gaining on the wagon, attempted to jump upon it, but "owing to Mr. Green's rapid driving, failed to reach the load."[11]

9. Ibid.
10. Ibid.
11. Ibid.

Along a wintry Bald Eagle Mountain Road – another view. Both sides of the road are still densely forested; perhaps not as thickly as when the minister and his wife walked this way when going to and coming from their Sunday church services.

There was another veteran woodsman of the olden time who would support the claims that a panther does scream, and that those screams are not attributable to screech owls. Philip Tome, in his classic treatise titled *Pioneer Life, or Thirty Years a Hunter*, recalls his personal hunting experiences in the Black Forest of northern Pennsylvania. In that treatise he records an instance that occurred one snowy November night after he had just shot a bear and had dragged its carcass under the protection of a projecting rock.

He was grateful for the shield from winter winds that the overhanging shelter provided, but then this feeling of security was dispelled "about nine o'clock" when two panthers made their presence known. "Finding what was perhaps their usual quarters invaded, they set up a screaming that would have sent the blood to the stoutest heart," recalled Tome. "I took my gun in one hand, my tomahawk in the other, while my dog stood near me, and I resolved, should they attack me, to give them a warm reception. They kept up their fearful serenade until midnight, when they withdrew, and I heard no more of them."[12]

NOTE: The last panther bounty paid in Pennsylvania, according to *Williamsport Post Gazette* newspaper articles on Pennsylvania panther sightings, dated 07/03/1895 and 08/18/1903, was made to John Lucas in 1886, who shot the panther in the Moshannon Valley region on the border of Centre and Clearfield Counties.

---

12. Philip Tome, *Pioneer Life or Thirty Years a Hunter*, 171 ff.

BIBLIOGRAPHY

Africa, J. Simpson, *History of Huntingdon and Blair Counties, Pennsylvania*, Philadelphia, Louis H. Everts, 1883.

Aldrich, Lewis Cass, *History of Clearfield County, Pennsylvania*, Syracuse, NY, D. Mason and Company, 1887.

Allen, J. A., "Occurrence of the Buffalo in Union County, Pennsylvania, *Memoirs of the Museum of Comparative Zoology* subtitled *The American Bisons Living and Extinct*, Cambridge, MA, Harvard University Press, 1876.

Ashe, Thomas, *Travels in America Performed in 1806*, London, William Sawyer and Company, 1808.

Bates, Samuel P., *History of Greene County, Pennsylvania*, Chicago, Nelson, Rishforth and Company, 1888.

Bell, Herbert C., *History of Northumberland County, Pennsylvania*, Chicago, Brown, Runk, and Company, Publishers, 1891.

Boucher, J. N., *History of Westmoreland County, Pennsylvania*, New York and Chicago, Lewis Publishing Company, 1906.

Blackman, Emily C., *History of Susquehanna County, Pennsylvania*, Philadelphia, Claxton, Remsen and Haffelfinger, 1873.

Browning, Meshach, *Forty-four Years of the Life of a Hunter*, reprint of the 1859 edition, Baltimore, Gateway Press, Inc., 1993.

Centre County Historical Society, *Centre County Heritage, 1956–75*, (compilation of twenty years of the society's quarterly publication of the same name), Bellefonte, PA, 1975.

Coco, Gregory, *On the Bloodstained Field*, Gettysburg, PA, Thomas Publications, 1987.

Commonwealth of Pennsylvania, *Pennsylvania at Chickamauga and Chattanooga*, Harrisburg, PA, W. S. Ray, state printer, 1900.

Craft, David, *History of Bradford County Pennsylvania*, L. H. Everts and Company, 1878.

Davis, W. W. H., *The History of Bucks County Pennsylvania*, Doylestown, PA, Democrat Book and Job Office, 1876.

Day, Sherman, *Historical Collections of the State of Pennsylvania*, Port Washington, NY, Ira J. Friedman, 1843.

Doddridge, Joseph, *Notes on the Settlement and Indian Wars of the Western Parts of Virginia and Pennsylvania*, Wellsburgh, VA, Wellsburgh Virginia Gazette, 1824.

Donehoo, Dr. George P., *History of Indian Village and Place Names in Pennsylvania*, Harrisburg, PA, The Telegraph Press, 1928.

Dubbs, Paul, M., *Where to Go and Place-Names of Centre County*, State College, PA, Nittany Printing and Publishing Company, 1961.

Egle, William H. *History of Pennsylvania*, Harrisburg, PA, De Witt C. Goodrich and Company, 1876.

Ellis, Franklin, and Austin N. Hungerford, *History of the Susquehanna and Juniata Valleys (Pennsylvania)*, Philadelphia, Everts, Peck, and Richards, 1886.

Fletcher, Stevenson W., *Pennsylvania Agricultural and Country Life, 1640–1840*, Harrisburg, PA, Pennsylvania Historical and Museum Commission, 1971.

Gibson, J. T., *History of the Seventy-eighth Pennsylvania Volunteer Infantry*, Pittsburgh, PA, Pittsburgh Printing Company, 1905.

Grimm, Herbert L., and Paul L. Roy, *Human Interest Stories of the Three Days' Battles at Gettysburg*, Gettysburg, PA, Times and News Publishing Company, 1927.

Guilday, John E., "Evidence for Buffalo In Prehistoric Pennsylvania," appeared in the *Pennsylvania Archeologist, September 1963, Volume 33 (#3)*.

Hain, H. H., *History of Perry County, Pennsylvania*, Harrisburg, PA, Hain-Moore Company, 1922.

Hardwick, Charles, *Traditions, Superstitions, and Folk-lore, (Chiefly Lancashire and the North of England)*, Manchester, England, A. Ireland and Company, 1872.

Harting, James E., *Extinct British Animals*, London, Trubner and Company, 1880.

Heckewelder, Rev. John, *History, Manner, and Customs of the Indian Nations*, Philadelphia, Lippincott's Press, 1876.

Henretta, J. E., *Kane and the Upper Allegheny*, Philadelphia, Winston and Company, 1929.

Heverley, Clement F., *Pioneer and Patriot Families of Bradford County, Pennsylvania, 1770–1800* Towanda, PA, Bradford Star Print, 1915.

Hollister, H., *History of the Lackawanna Valley*, Scranton, PA, M. Norton, bookseller and stationer, third edition, 1875.

Ingram, John H., *The Haunted Homes and Family Traditions of Great Britain*, London, Reeves and Turner, 1905.

Jones, Uriah J., *History of the Early Settlement of the Juniata Valley*, Harrisburg, PA, Harrisburg Publishing Company, 1889.

Kauffman, Duane S., *Mifflin County Amish and Mennonite Story, 1791–1991*, Elverson, PA, Mifflin County Mennonite Historical Society, 1991.

Kieffer, Harry M., *Recollections of a Drummer Boy*, Houghton, Mifflin and Company, Boston and NY, 1883.

Korson, George, *Pennsylvania Songs and Legends*, Baltimore, Johns Hopkins Press, 1949.

Kraybill, Spencer, *Pennsylvania's Pine Creek Valley and Pioneer Families*, Baltimore, Gateway Press, 1991.

Kuhns, Oscar, *The German and Swiss Settlements of Colonial Pennsylvania*, New York, Henry Holt and Company, 1901.

Lazenby, Mary E., *Herman Husband: A Story of His Life, 1724–1795*, Washington DC, Old Neighborhood Press, 1940.

Leeson, Michael A., *History of the Counties of McKean, Elk, and Forest Pennsylvania*, Chicago, J. H. Beers and Company, 1890.

Linn, John Blair, *History of Centre and Clinton Counties, Pennsylvania*, Philadelphia, Louis H. Everts Company, 1883.

Lyman, Robert R. Sr., *History of Roulet Pa. and the Life of Burrel Lyman (The Founder)*, Coudersport, PA, Potter County Historical Society, 1967.

McClure, Alexander K., *Old-Time Notes of Pennsylvania*, John C. Winston Company, Philadelphia, 1905.

McKnight, W. J., *Pioneer Outline History of Northwestern Pennsylvania*, Philadelphia, Lippincott Company, 1905.

Meginness, John F., *Otzinachson, A History of the West Branch Valley*, Williamsport, PA, Gazette Printing House, 1889.

Mitchell, Edwin V., *It's an Old Pennsylvania Custom*, New York, Vanguard Press, Inc., 1947.

Montgomery, Thomas L., editor, *Frontier Forts of Pennsylvania*, Harrisburg, PA, Pennsylvania Historical Commission, 1916.

Muffly, Adjt. J. W., editor, *The Story of Our Regiment, A History of the 148th Pa. Volunteers*, Des Moines, IA, Kenyon Printing, 1904.

O'Hara, Mike, *Origins of Town Names of Northeast Pennsylvania*, Scranton, PA, Privately published by the author, 2017.

Old Home Week Committee, *Historical Souvenir of Lewistown, Penna.*, Lewistown, PA, The Sentinel Company, 1925.

Parkman, Francis, *The Conspiracy of Pontiac, Volume 1*, 6th edition, Boston, Little, Brown, and Company, 1870.

Pennsylvania Writers' Project, *Pennsylvania—A Guide to the Keystone State*, New York, Oxford University Press, 1940.

Rhoads, Samuel N., *Mammals of Pennsylvania and New Jersey*, Lancaster, PA, Wickersham Printing Company, 1903.

Sassaman, Grant N., editor, *Pennsylvania, A Guide to the Keystone State*, Pennsylvania Writers' Project, New York, Oxford University Press, 1940.

Schenck, J. S., *History of Warren County, Pennsylvania*, New York, Mason and Company, 1887.

Sheads, Col. Jacob M., editor, *A Pictorial History of the Battle of Gettysburg*, Gettysburg, PA, TEM, Inc., 1978.

Sipe, C. Hale, *The Indian Chiefs of Pennsylvania*, Butler, PA, Ziegler Printing Company, 1927.

———, *The Indian Wars of Pennsylvania*, Harrisburg, PA, The Telegraph Press, 1931.

Smith, Robert Walker, *History of Armstrong County, Pennsylvania*, Chicago, Waterman, Watkins, and Company, 1883.

Storey, Henry Wilson, *History of Cambria County Pennsylvania*, NY and Chicago, The Lewis Publishing Company, 1907

Swetnam, George, *Pittsylvania Country*, New York, Duell, Sloan and Pearce, Inc., 1951.

Taber, Thomas T. III, *Muncy Valley Lifeline, the Life and Times of the Williamsport and North Branch Railroad*, Muncy, PA, self-published, 1972.

Tantaquidgeon, Gladys, *Folk Medicine of the Delaware*, Harrisburg, PA, Pennsylvania Historical and Museum Commission, 1972.

Tome, Phillip, *Pioneer Life, or Thirty Years a Hunter*, Baltimore, Gateway Press, 1989 (reprint of the 1854 edition).

Welfley, William H., *History of Bedford and Somerset Counties Pennsylvania*, Lewis Publishing Company, New York and Chicago, 1906.

Welfley, William H., E. Howard Blackburn, and William H. Koontz, *History of Bedford, Somerset, and Fulton Counties, Pennsylvania*, Chicago, Waterman and Watkins, 1884.

Withers, Alexander Scott, *Chronicles of Border Warfare*, Cincinnati, OH, Robert Clarke Company, 1895.

ABOUT THE AUTHOR

JEFFREY R. FRAZIER is a native of Centre Hall, Centre County. A 1967 graduate of Penn State University, BS degree in Science, he also holds an MBA in Finance from Rider University in New Jersey. He currently resides at 100 Hawknest Way, Graystone Court Villas—Apt. 135 Bellefonte, Pa., 16823. He can be reached via phone at 814-360-4401, or by email at jandhfra2@yahoo.com, or by contacting his publisher (Sunbury Press).

This Sunbury Press edition of *Volume VIII* of the author's *Pennsylvania Fireside Tales* series is a new edition and represents an expanded and improved version of all previous editions. Formatting has been improved, as well as number and quality of photos, but all the same tales that appeared in the original editions are included in this edition, along with new details added in some cases that were obtained after the last edition was published. Also, there is one new chapter not included in previous editions.